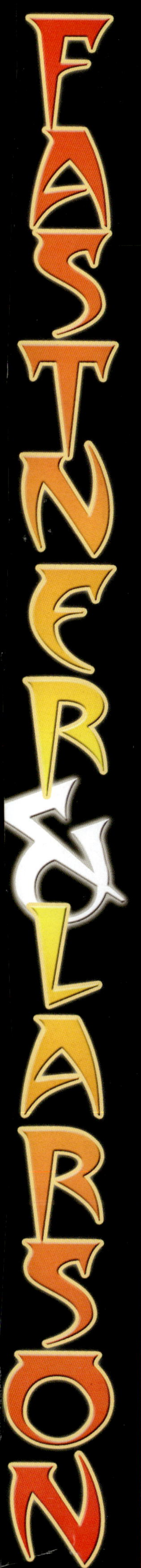

BEAUTIES & BEASTS

FASTNER
LARSON

AN SQP PRESENTATION

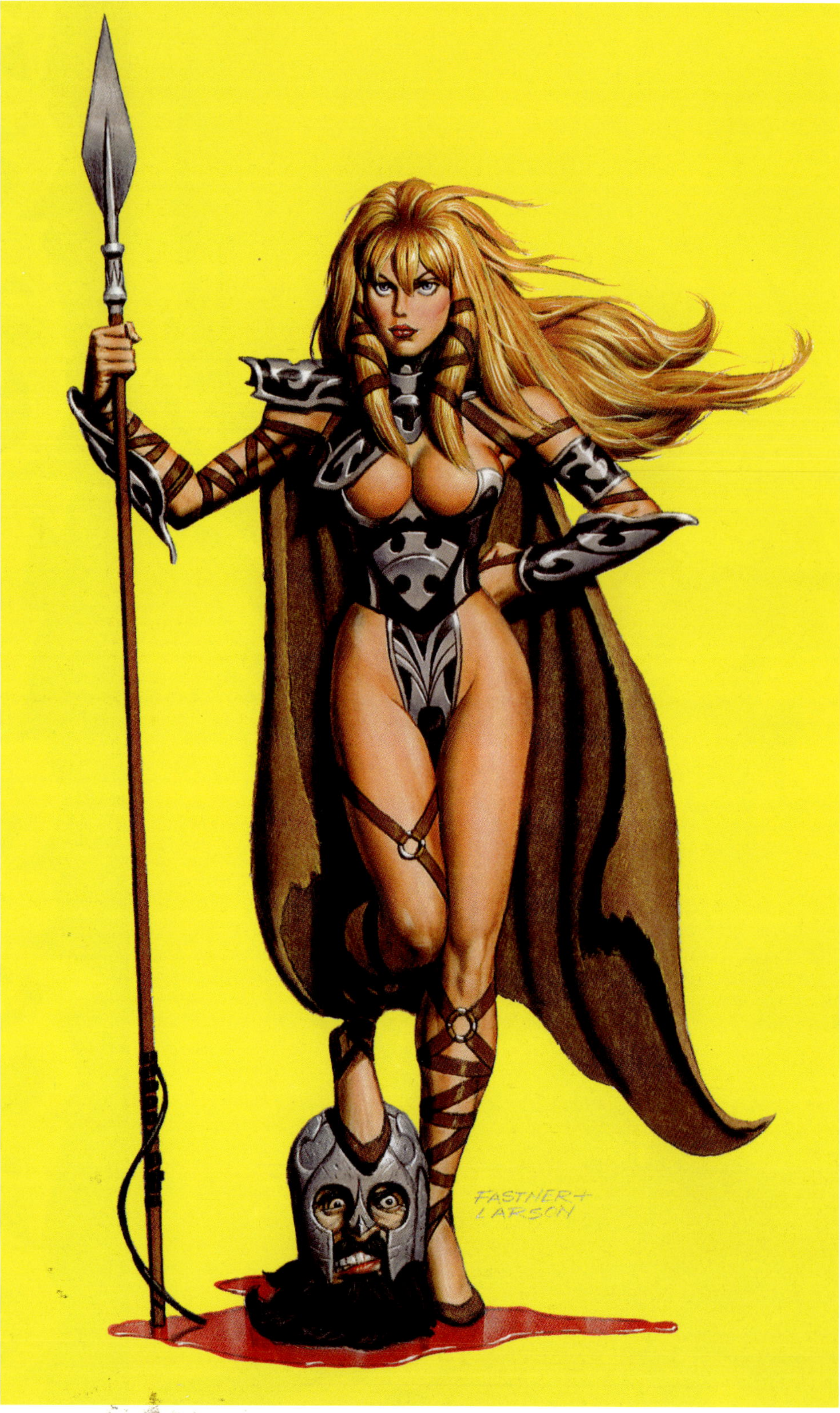

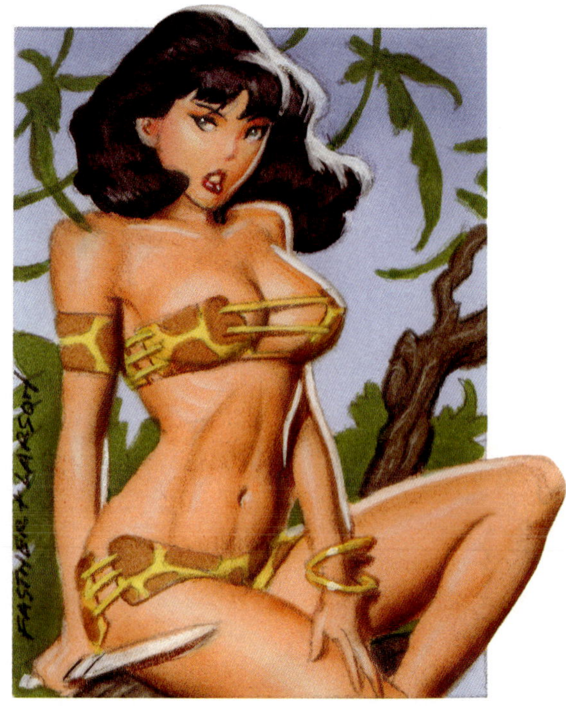

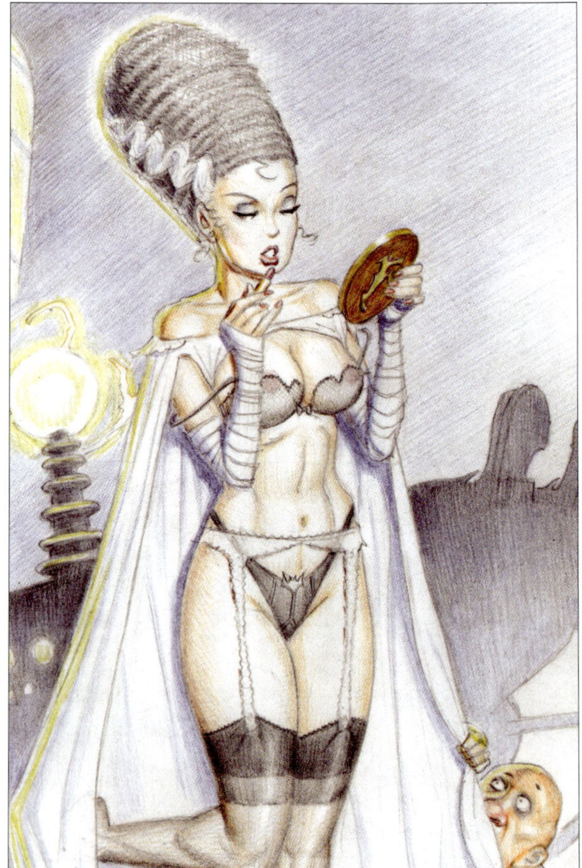

Fastner & Larson's Beauties & Beasts Vol 1

ISBN 978-0-86562-206-7 Printed in China.
Book design by Grassy Knoll Studios.
Distributed in Europe through www.fanfareuk.co.uk

Published by
SQP Inc.
PO Box 248 - Columbus, NJ 08022

Sal Quartuccio & Bob Keenan - Publishers

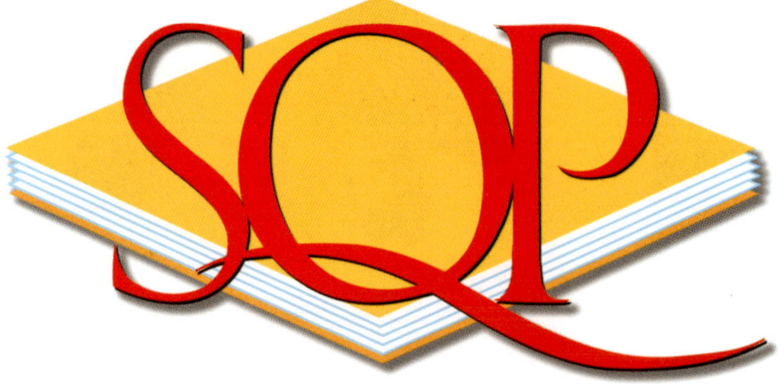

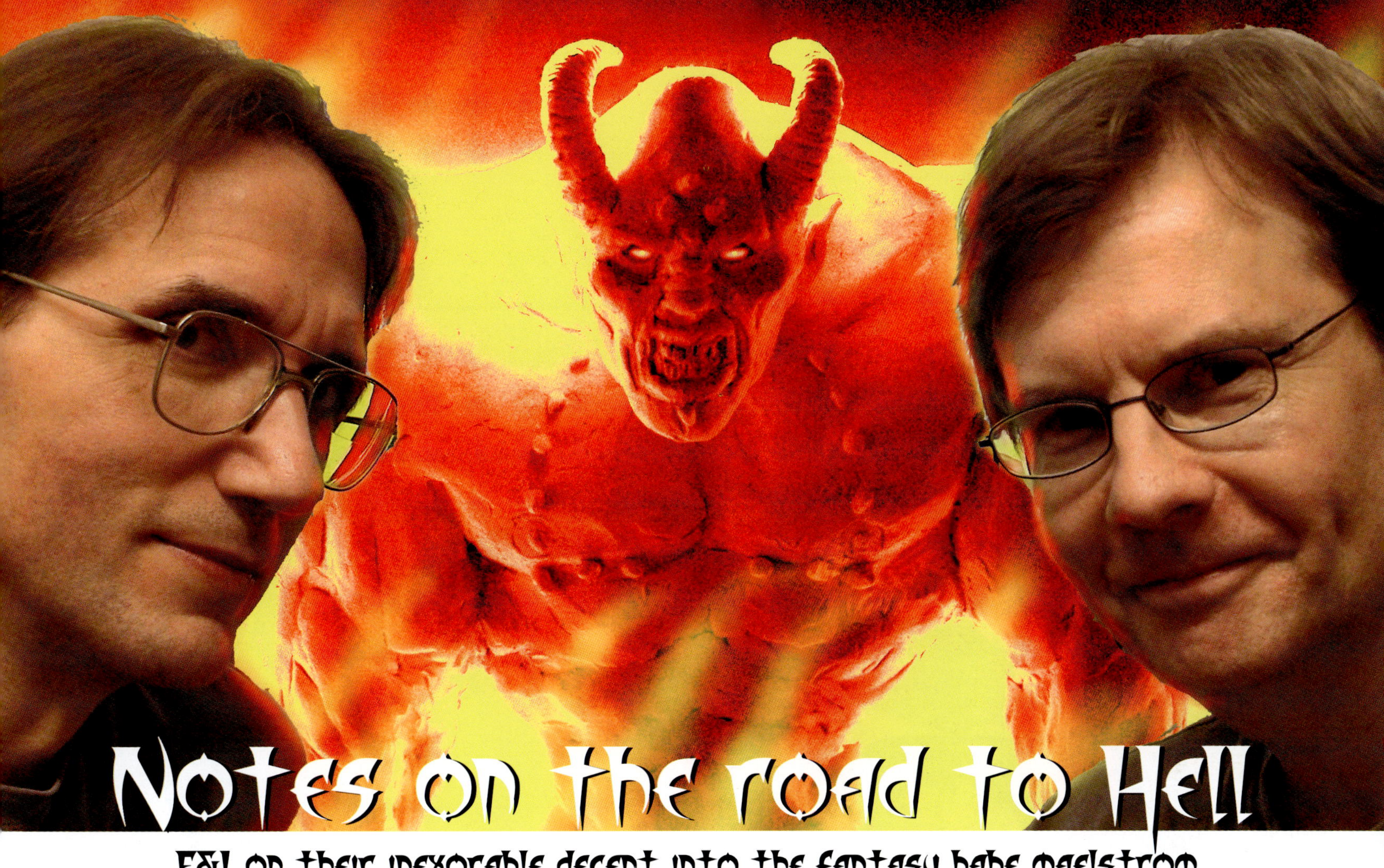

Notes on the road to Hell

F&L on their inexorable decent into the fantasy babe maelstrom

Let us (Steve and Rich, seen here conferencing with our, uh, investment banker) be the first to welcome you to the latest collection of F&L imagery.

Fantasy art comes in many flavors; *Beauties & Beasts* is yet another attempt to lead you off the path of cats-with-wings, and into the valley of girls who are just plain trouble, any way you slice it.

Before we get things going, a friendly heads-up for any stray devotees of a certain similarly named, universally beloved fairy tale. If you happened to have wandered in here based solely on our title – you know, not paying all that much attention to what's going on around you – just get up and go right now, because you're on the verge of taking your eyeballs out for a stroll in the wrongest of neighborhoods.

For those who are unfamiliar with our work, we've been painstaking contributors to the Decline of Western Civilization – aided and abetted by our publisher pals at SQP – since about 1976. Toothsome fantasy wenches, ooky monsters and strange doin's are our stock in trade.

If Bob & Sal's titles for our previous works (*Haunted House of Lingerie, Bed & Bondage*, and, if you think about it, *Tricks & Treats*) aren't a giveaway, a cursory examination of the present volume should make it clear: our particular road to hell is paved with anything but good intentions.

It's almost impossible, for example, to put a positive spin on something like "Young Man with a Paddle" (p.60), unless it might be the whole "family that flays together, stays together" angle.

Likewise, "Cattle Call" (p.51), which has a decidedly disturbing 50s pulp vibe, except for the nudity and the Korn fan, of course.

Ensconced among an assortment of similarly flat out, completely-off-our-tractor private commissions are some of Steve's disarmingly tasteful color pencil studies ("Mother Lode", p.34); our 1980 cover for Kevin Hancer's *Paperback Price Guide* ("He Who Glows", p.14); and a selection of our favorite grayscale portfolio plates, which Steve has lovingly repainted in digital color ("Night Slayers, p.39).

If that's not enough to tempt you into our crawl-space of infernal delights, we have a couple of surprises on hand as well, including our very own cat with wings. Sort of.

Steve Fastner
Rich Larson

Minneapolis
February, 2010

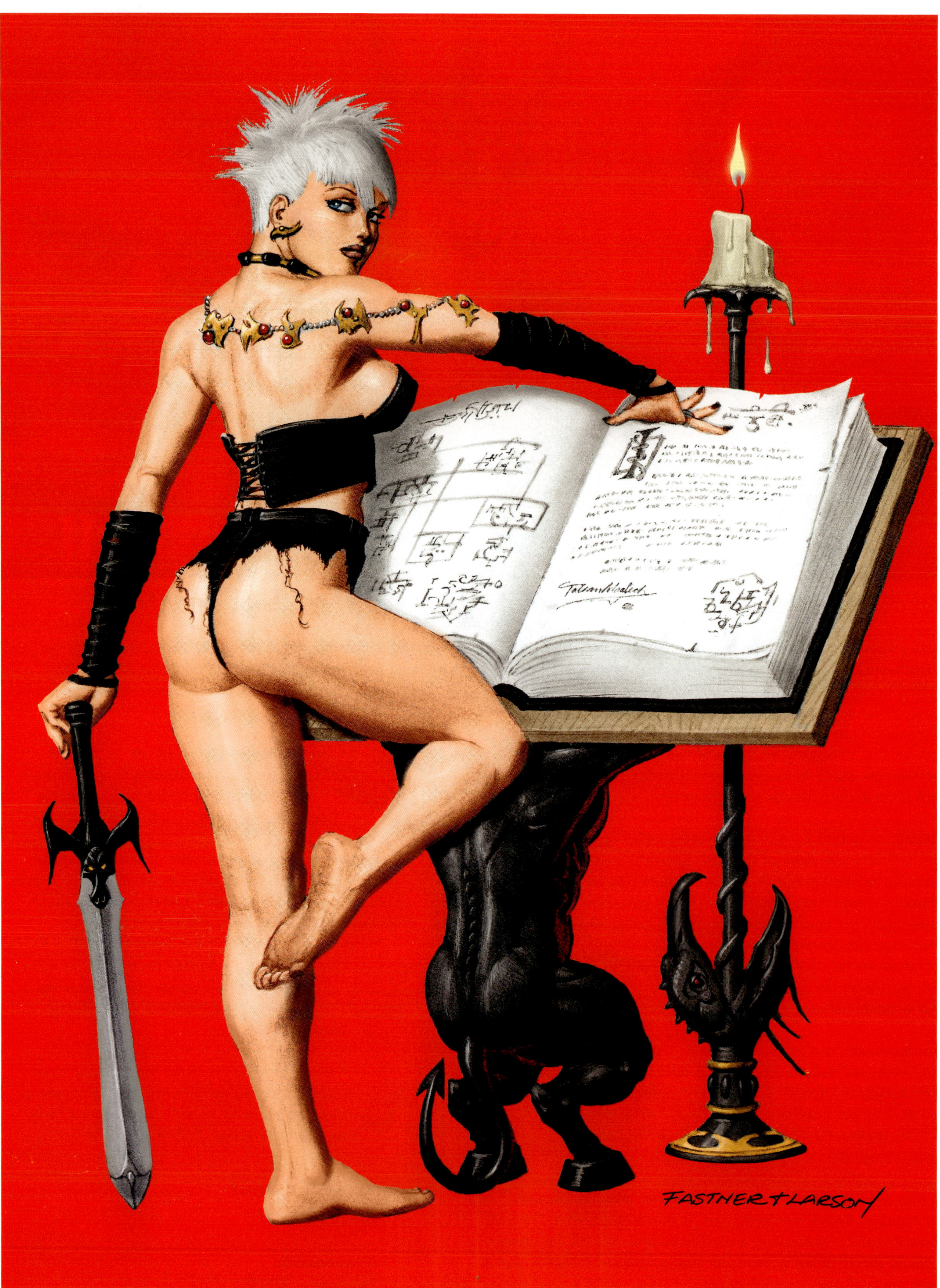

Belle, Book and Candle

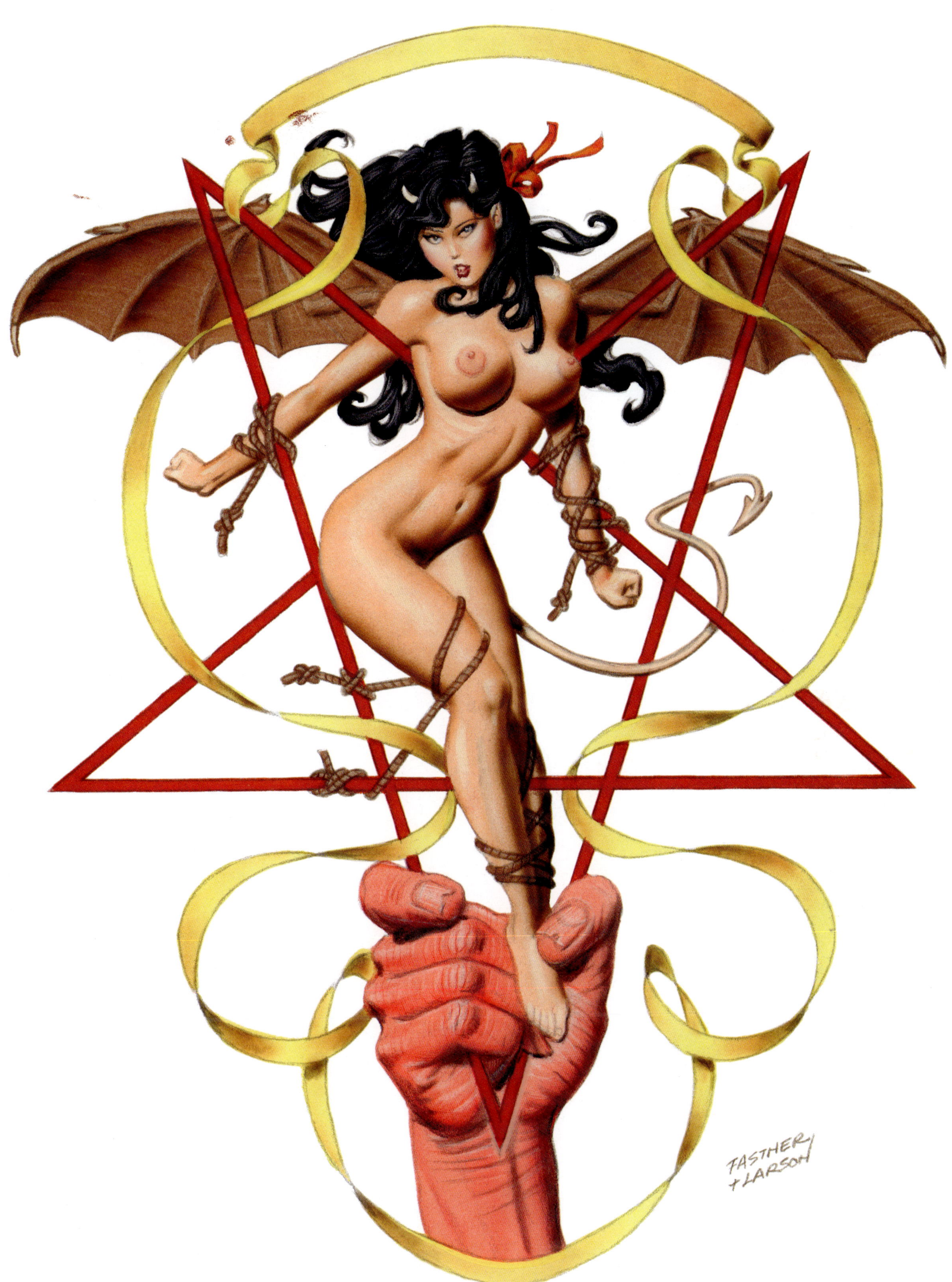

Starfallen

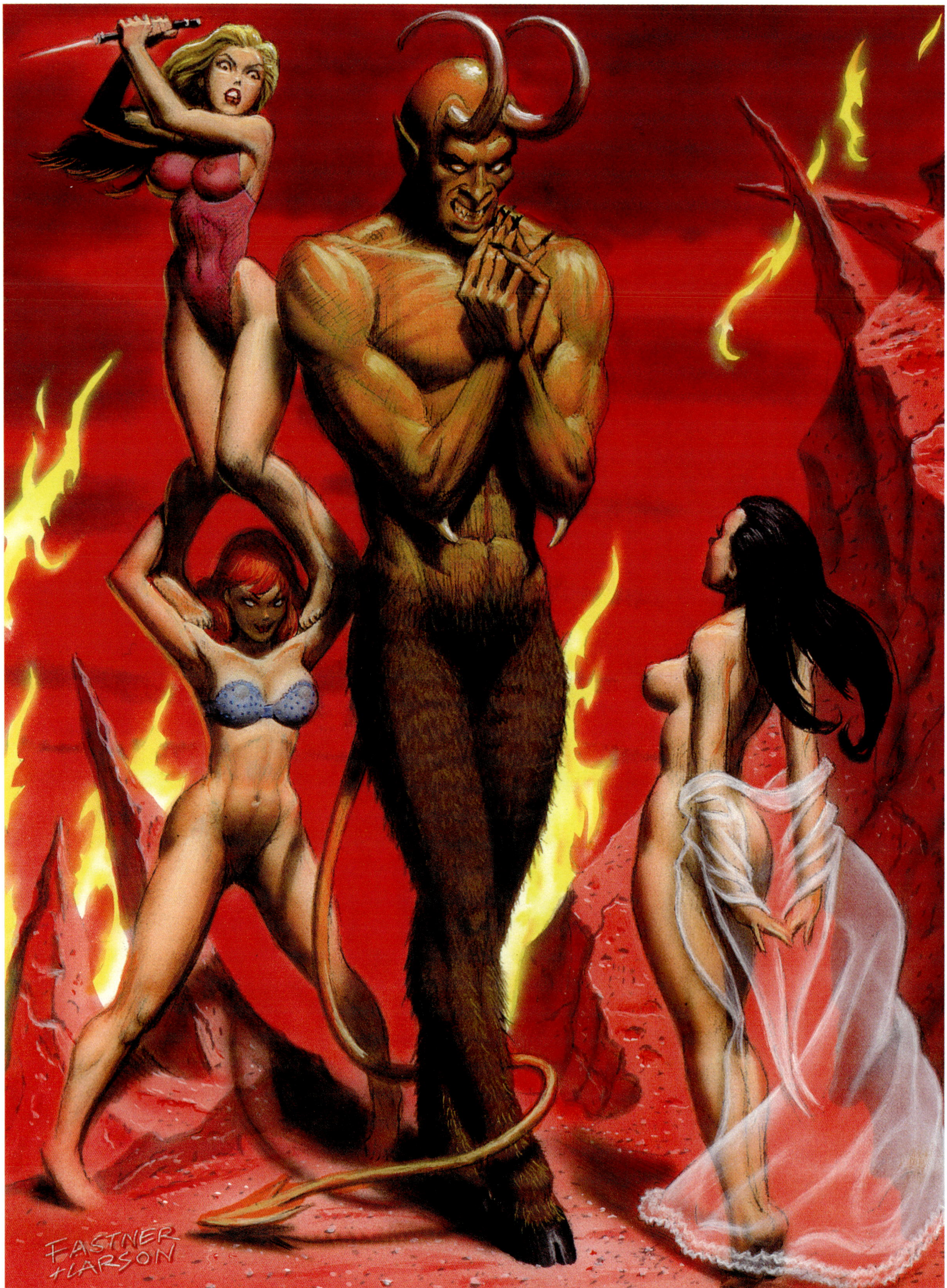

Plan "B"

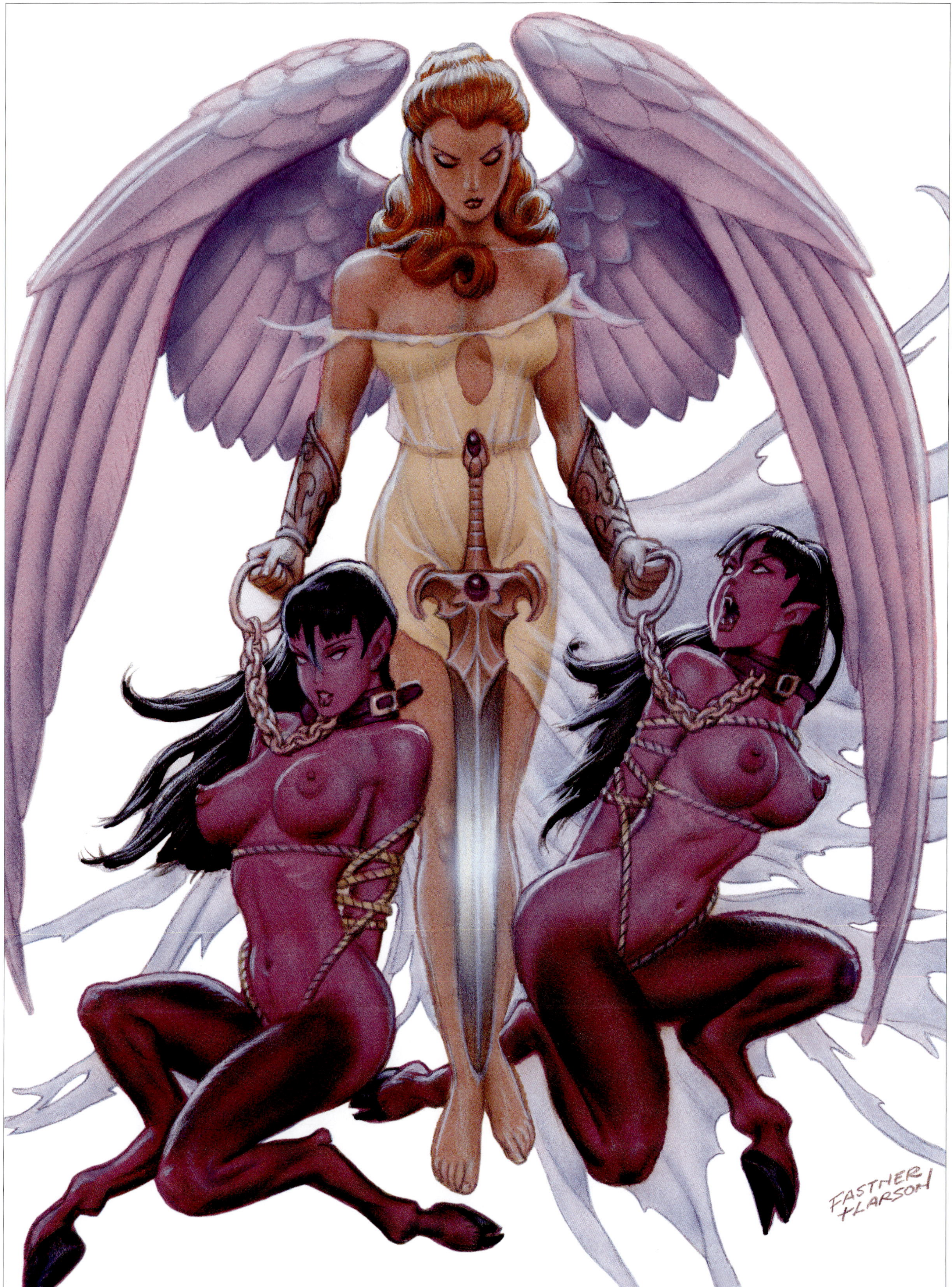

Dominion

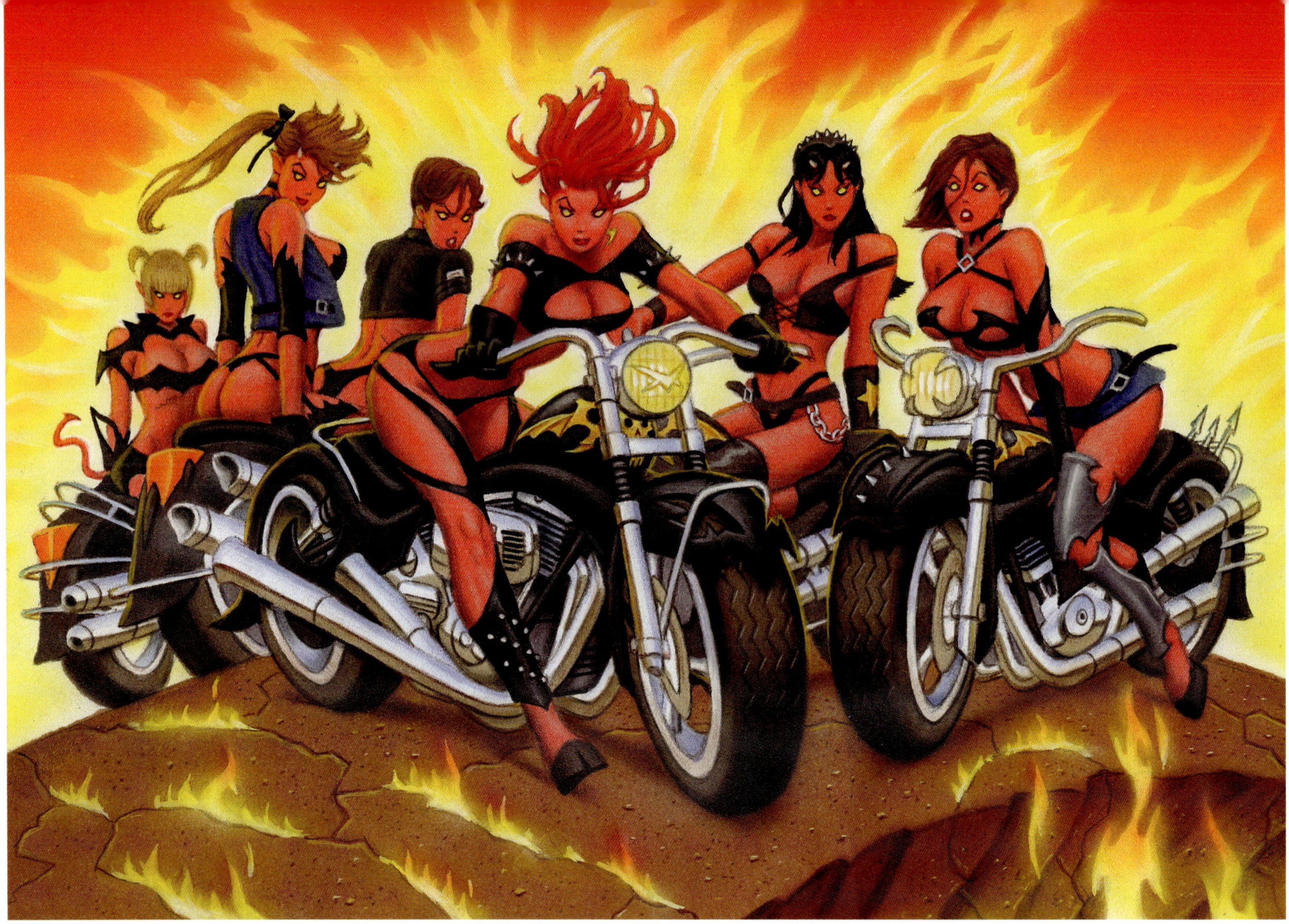

Girl's Club

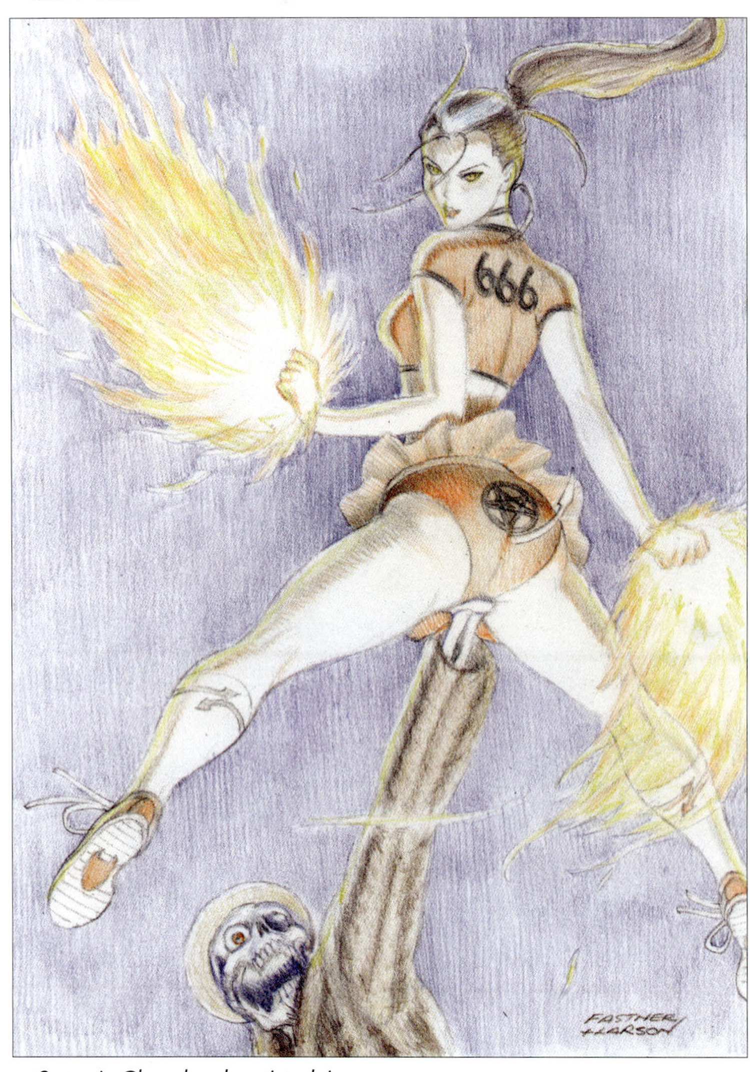

Satan's Cheerleaders (study)

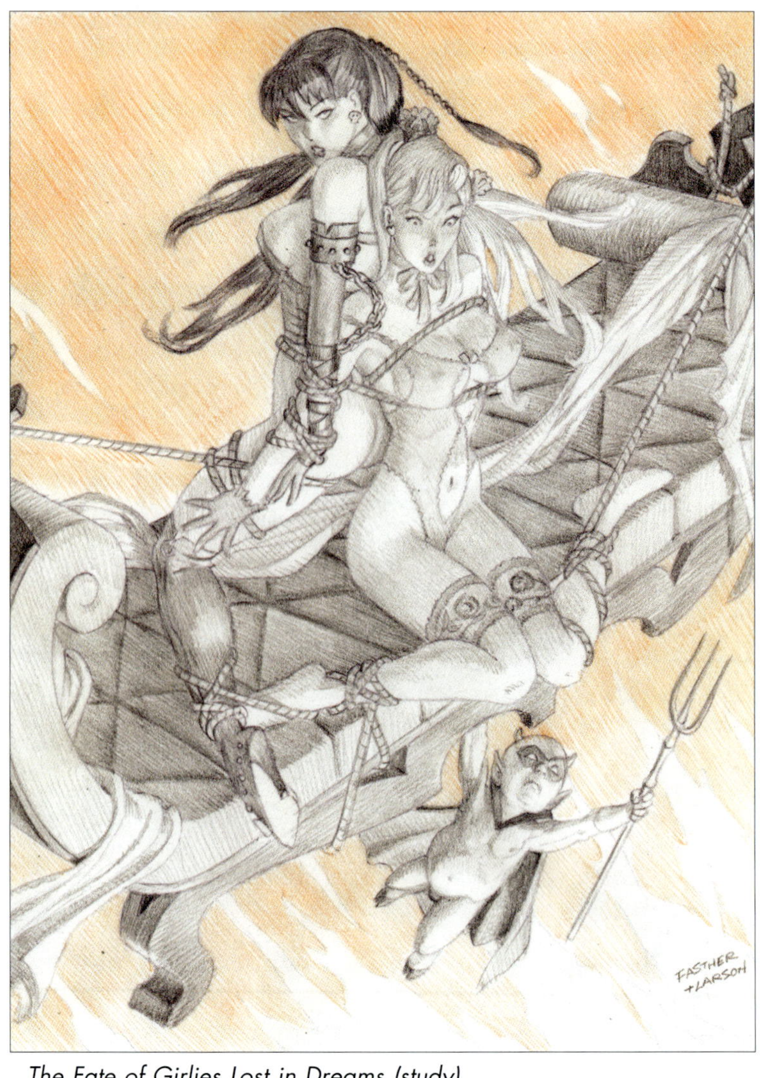

The Fate of Girlies Lost in Dreams (study)

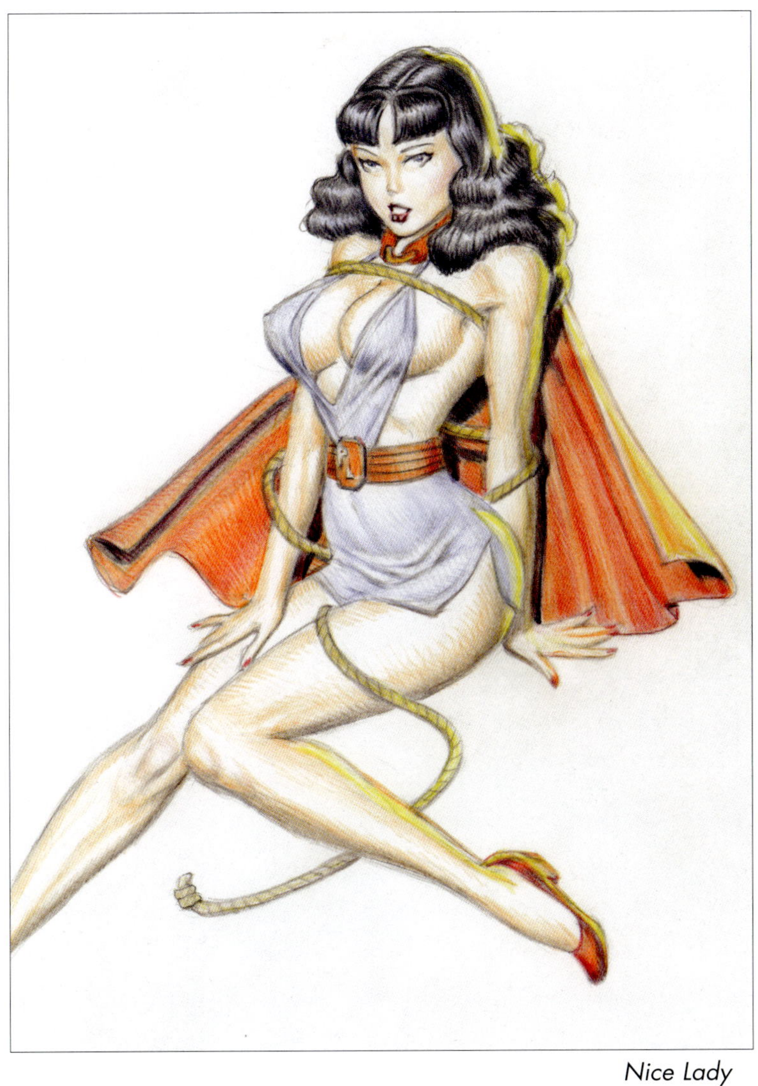

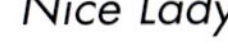
Nice Lady

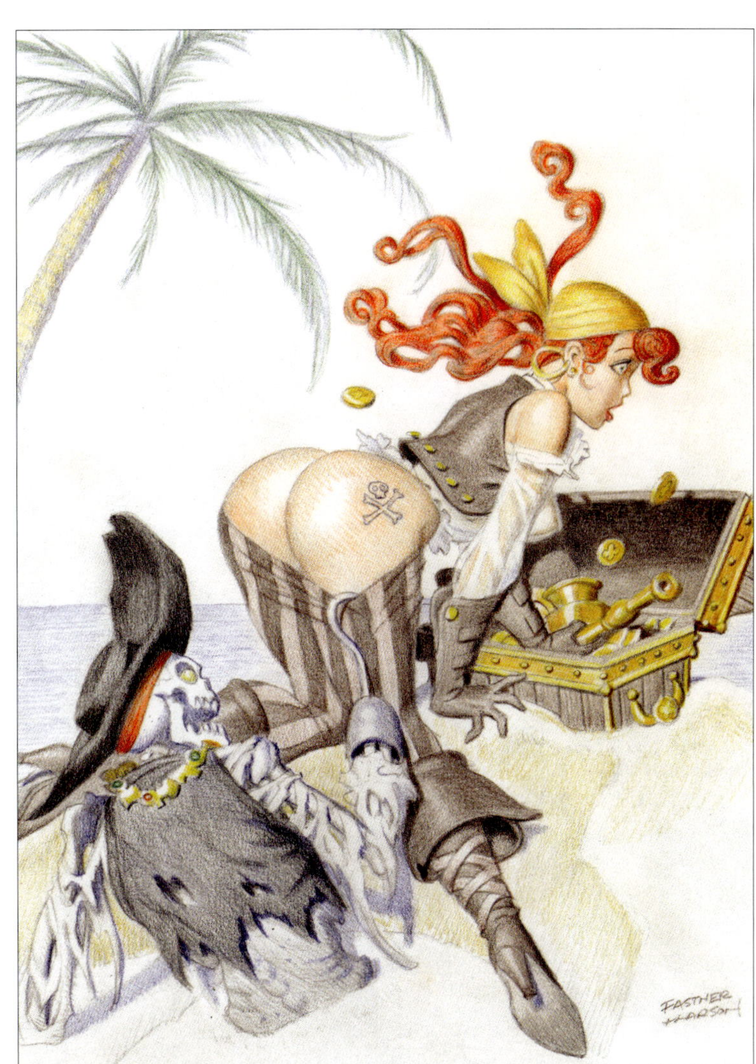

Booty (study)

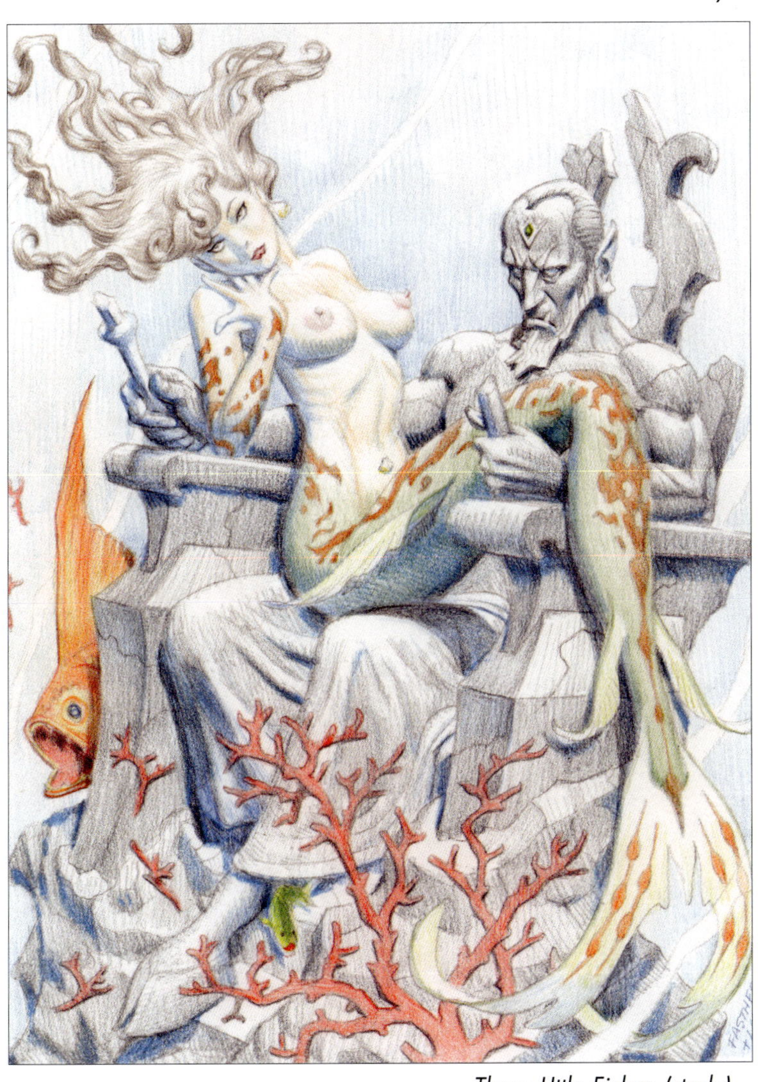

Three LIttle Fishes (study)

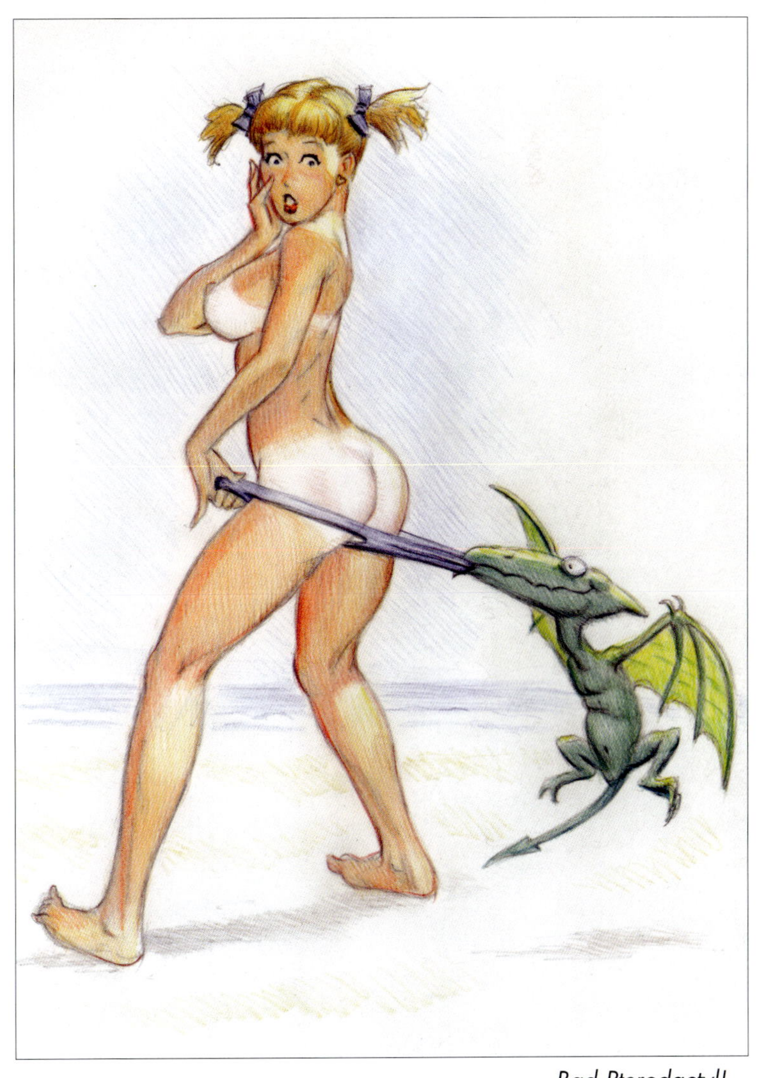

Bad Pterodactyl!

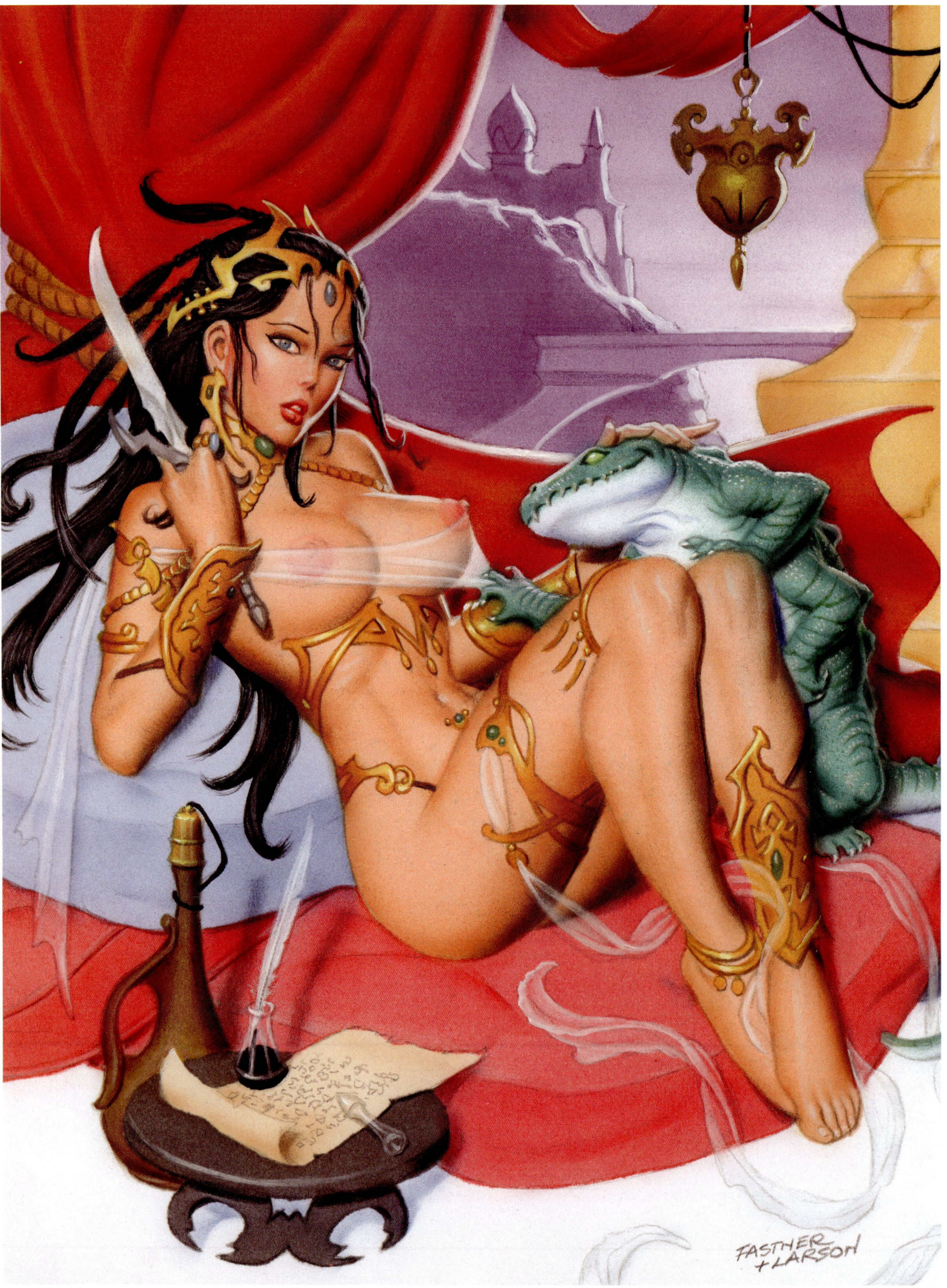

Princess & Pet

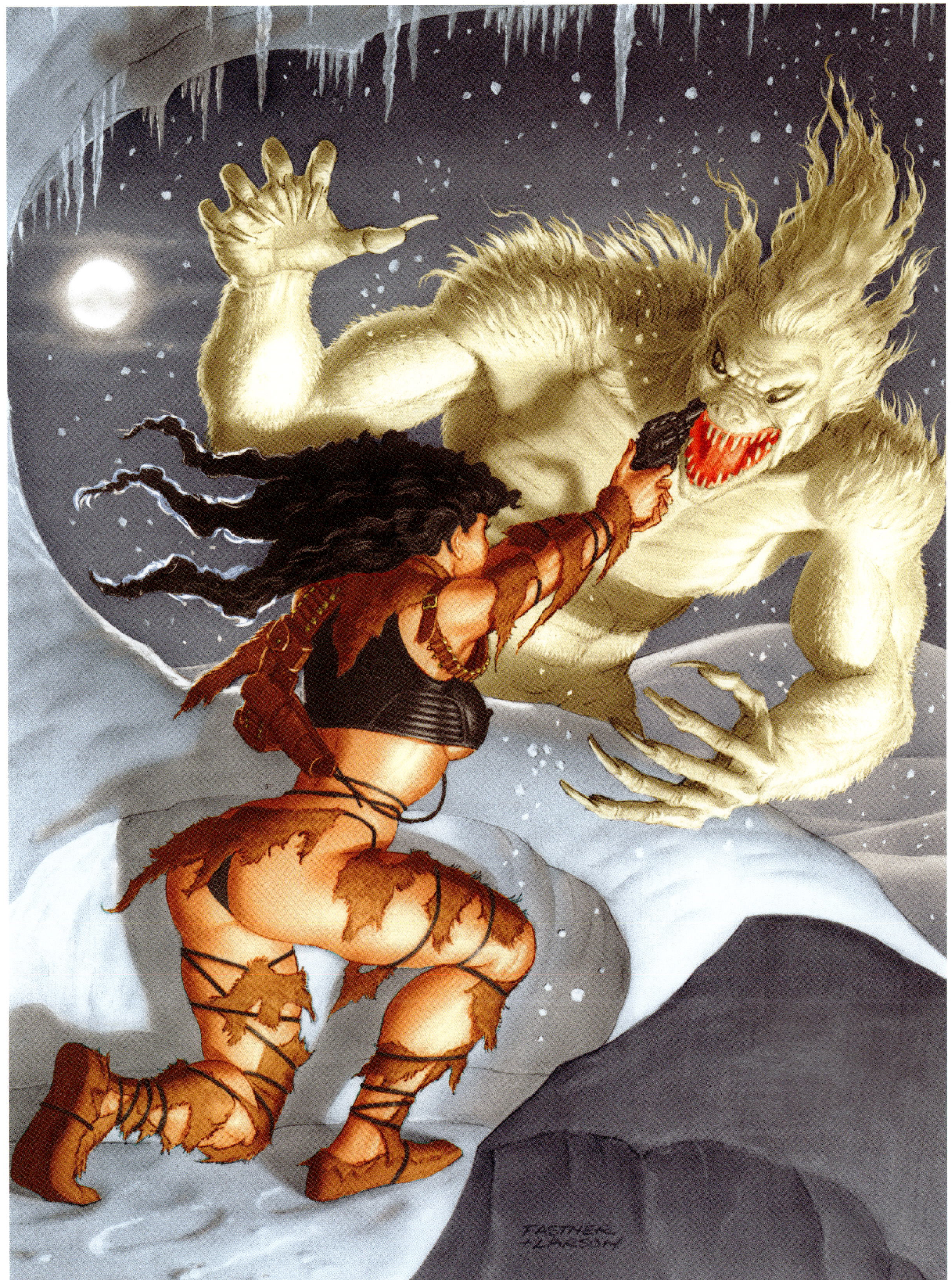

Snow Monster

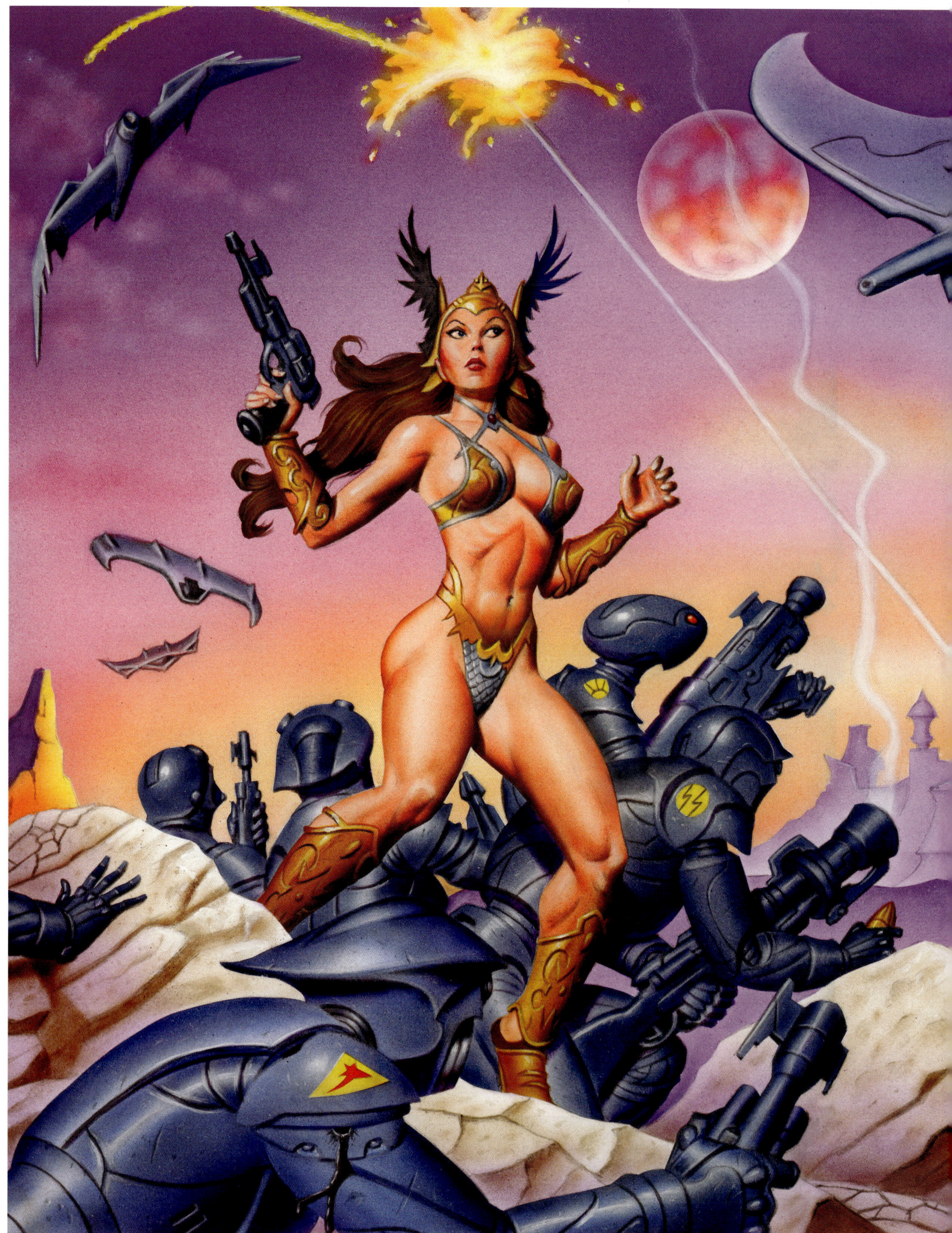

Robot Rebellion

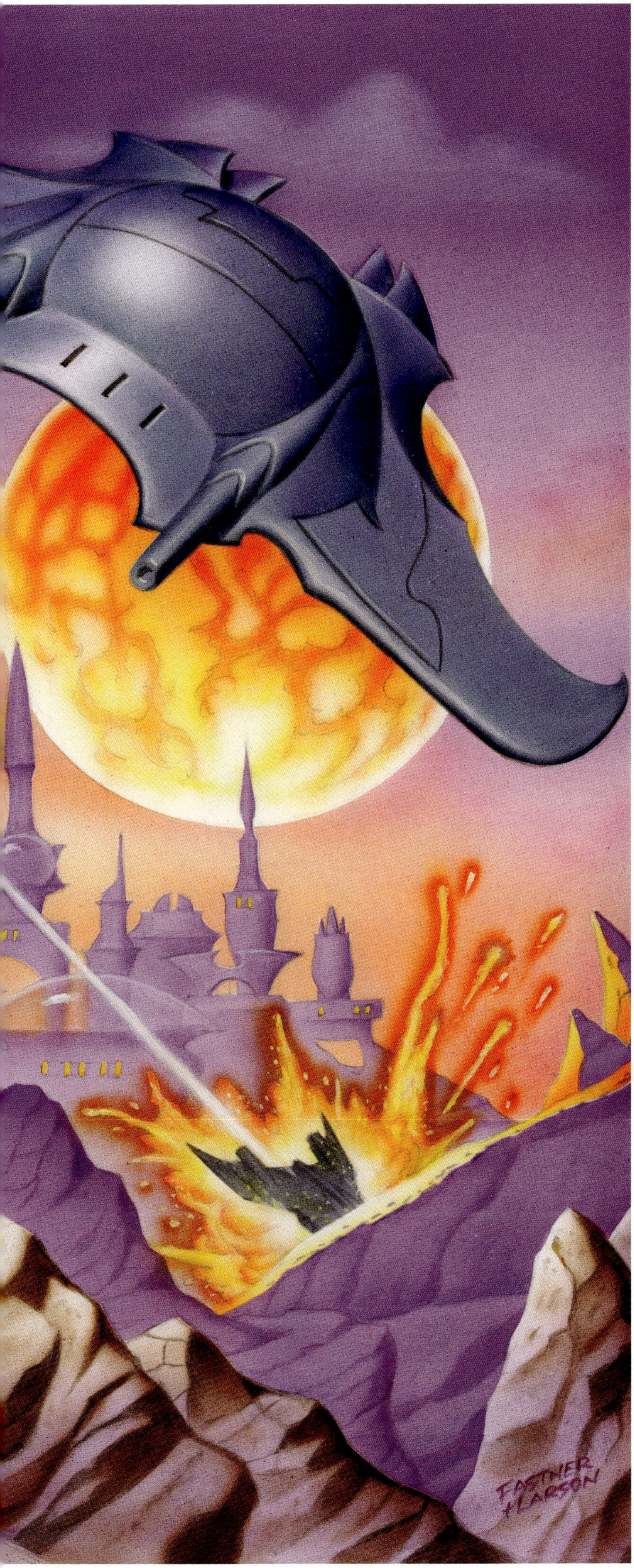

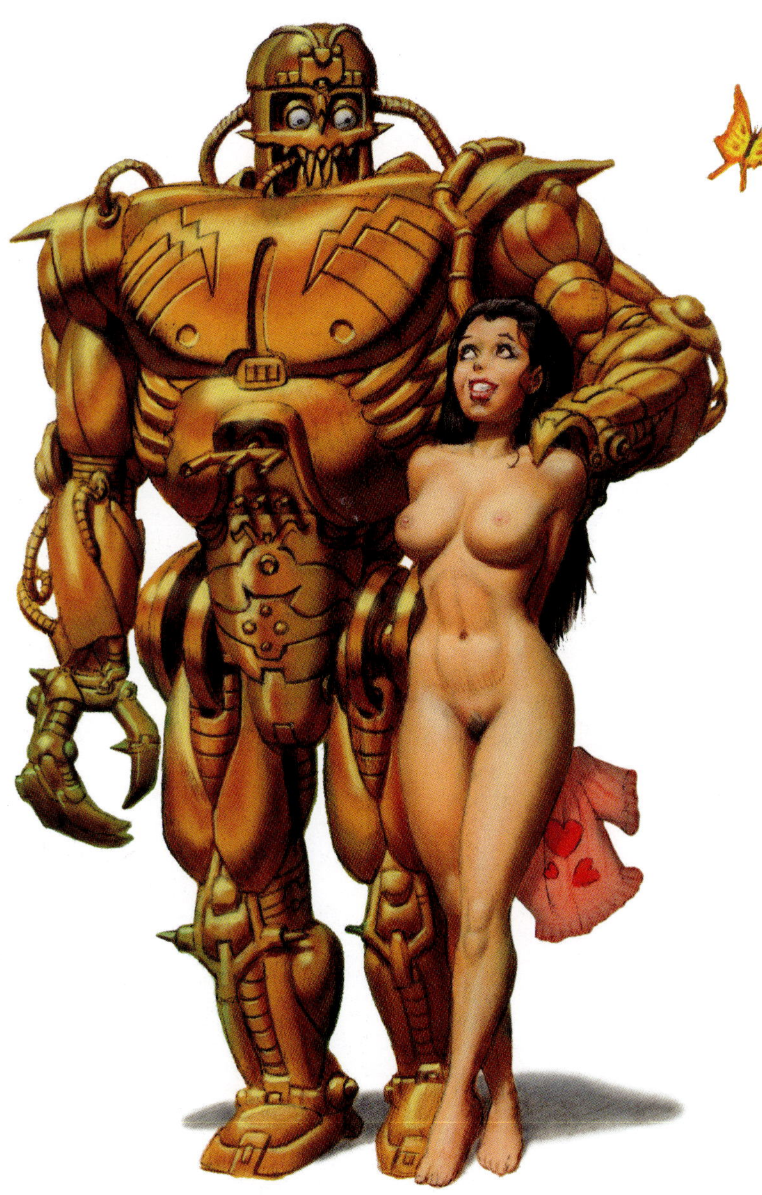

Girl and Her Robot

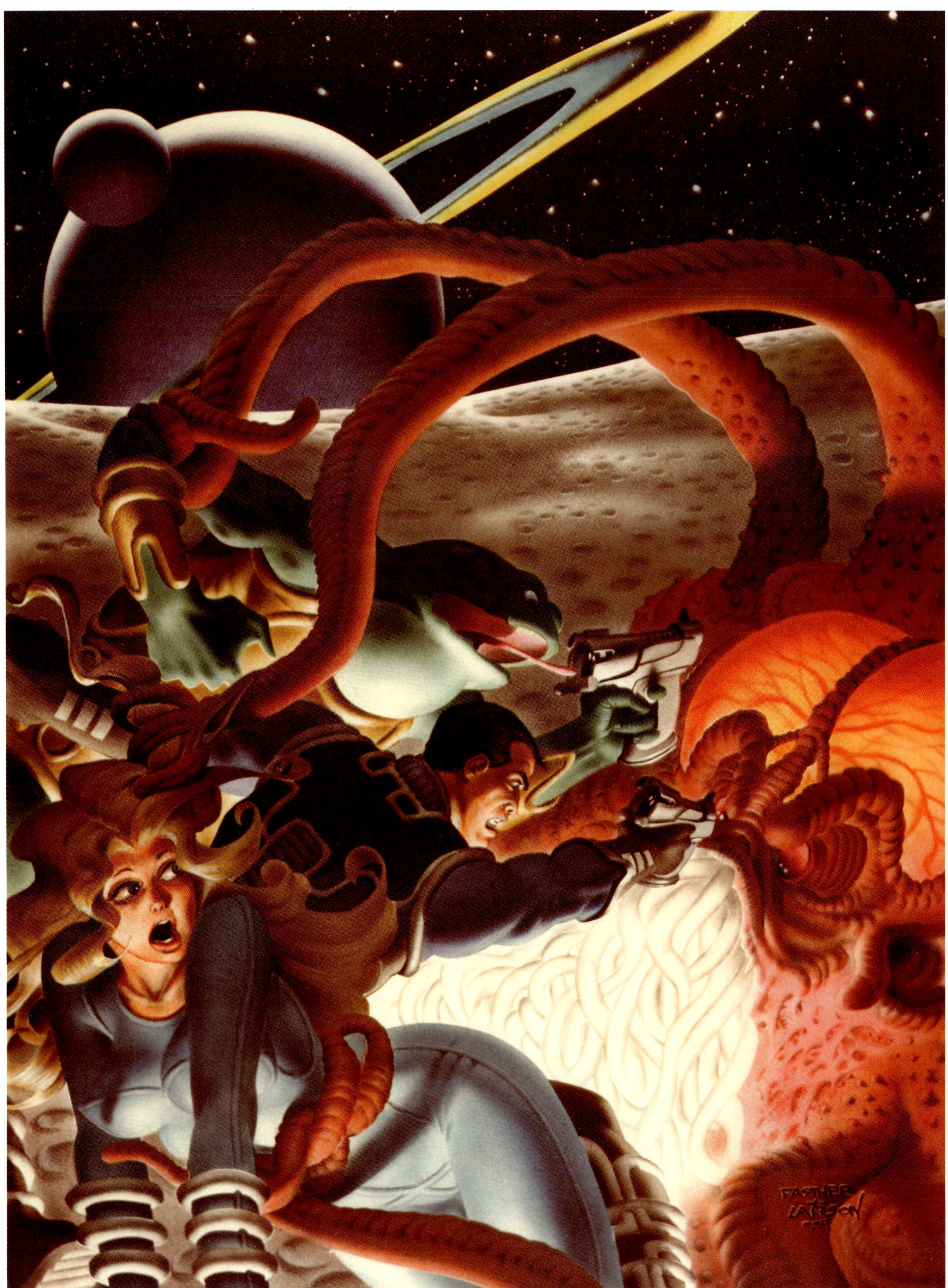

He Who Glows

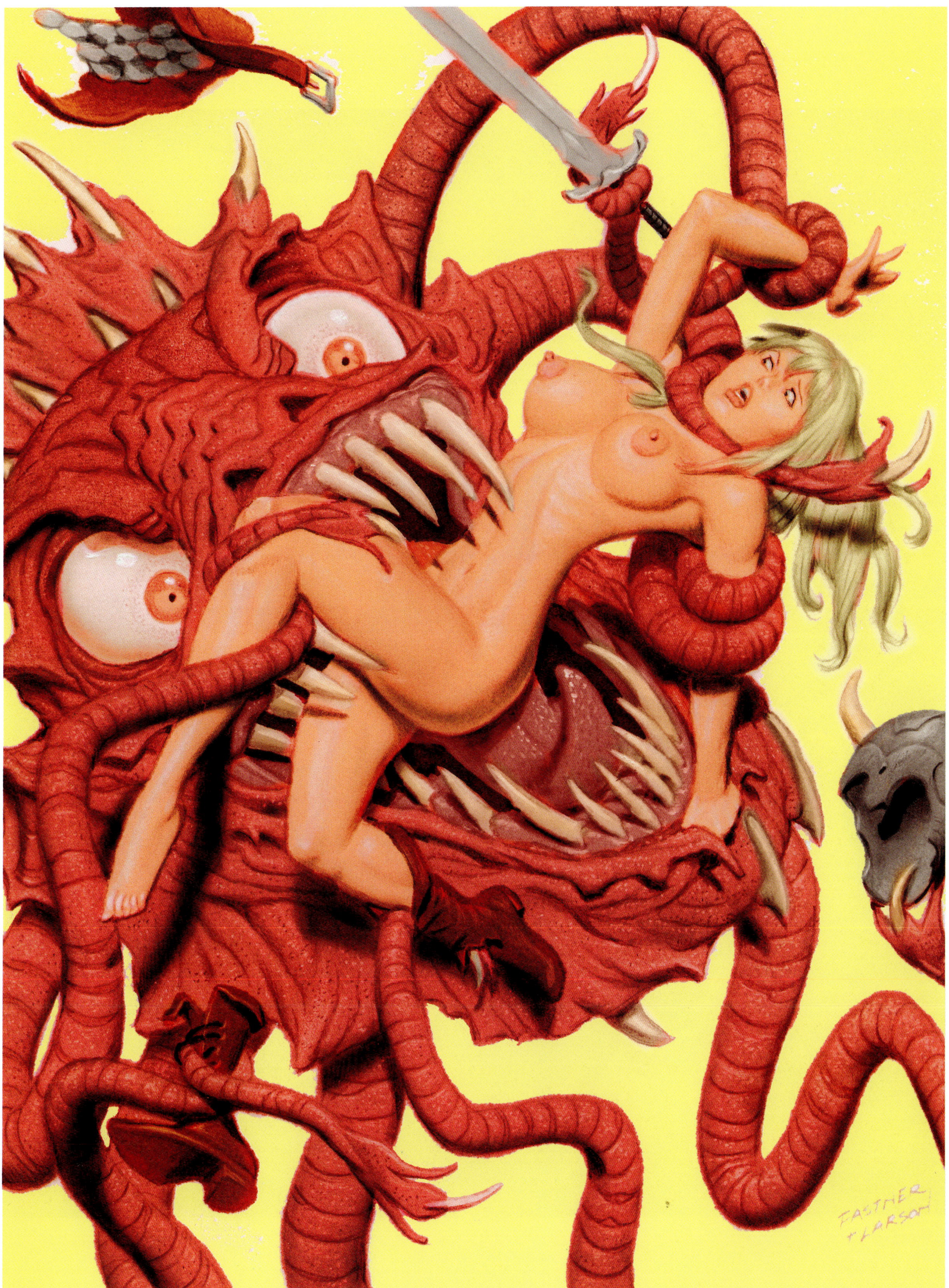

Tentacle Trouble

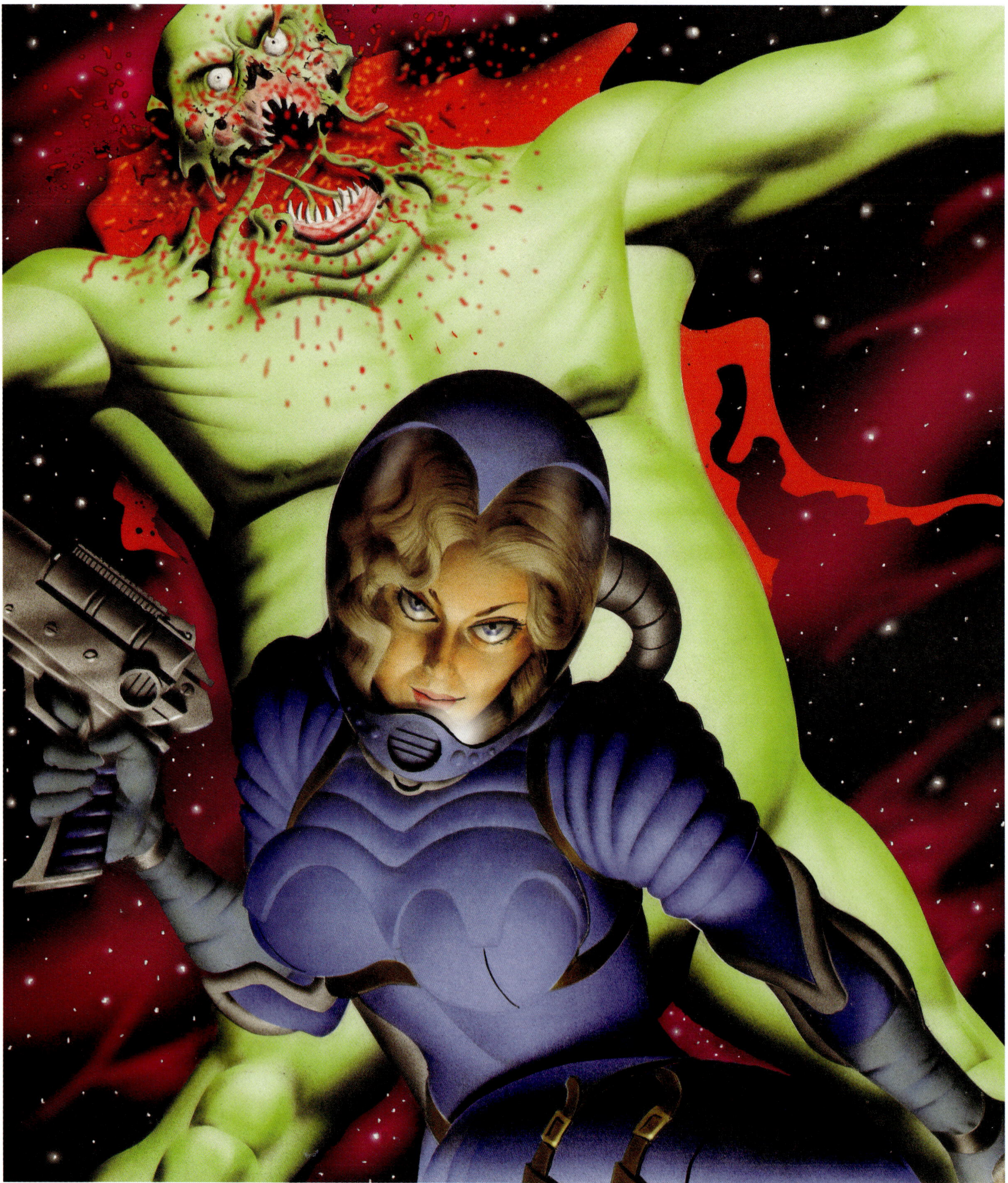

Green Death

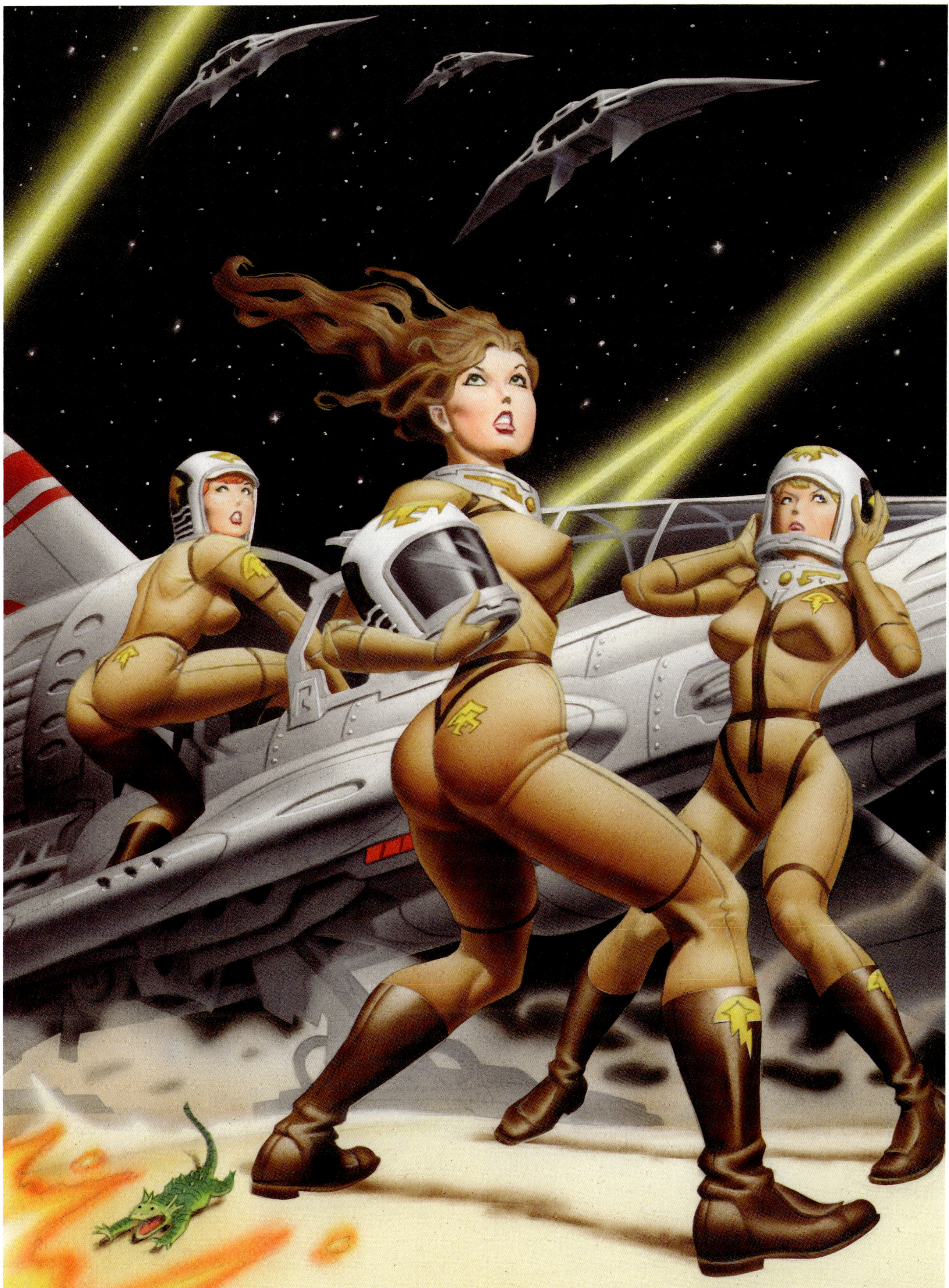

Space Jockeys

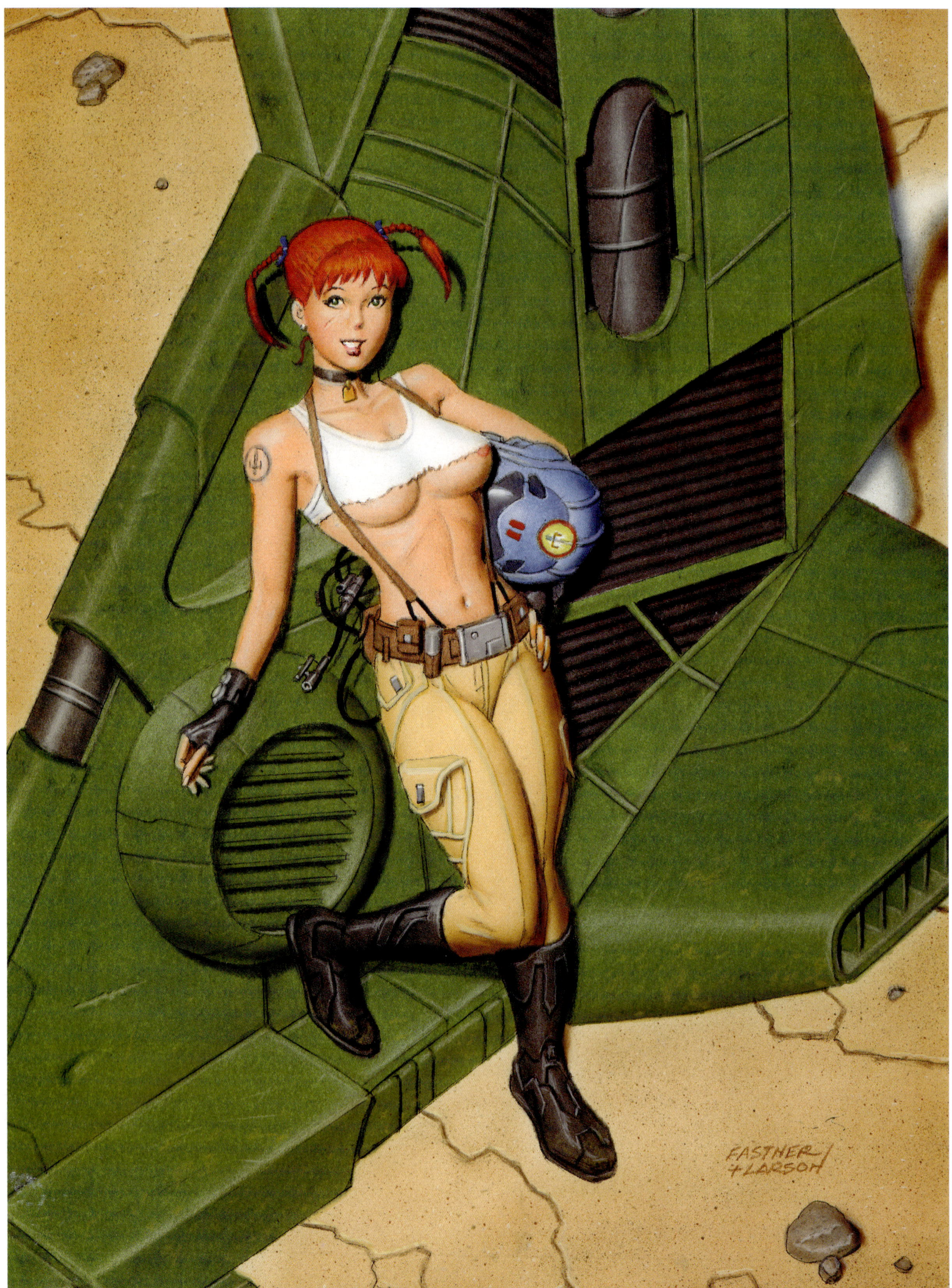

Mech Warrior

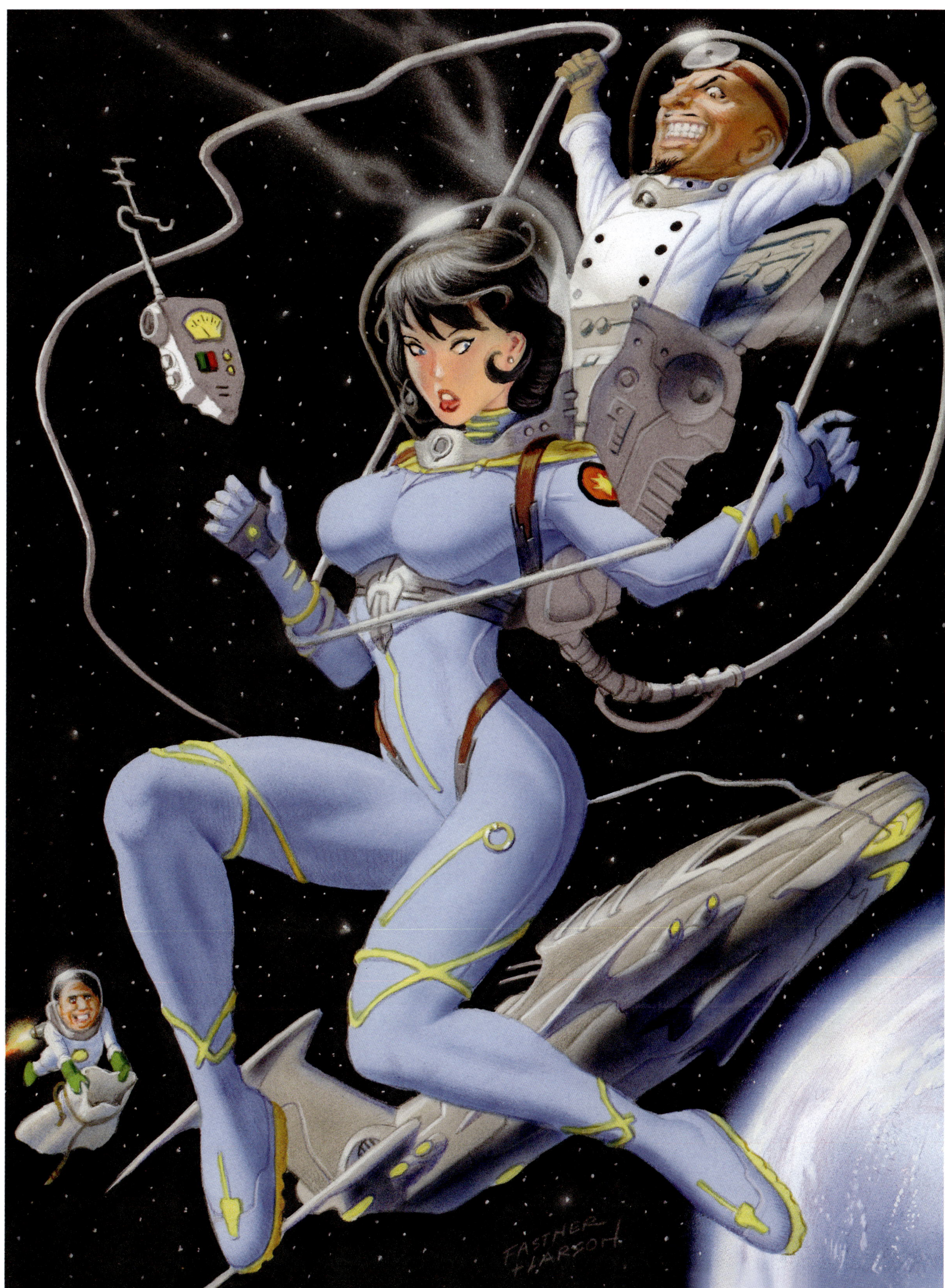

Space Thumbkin

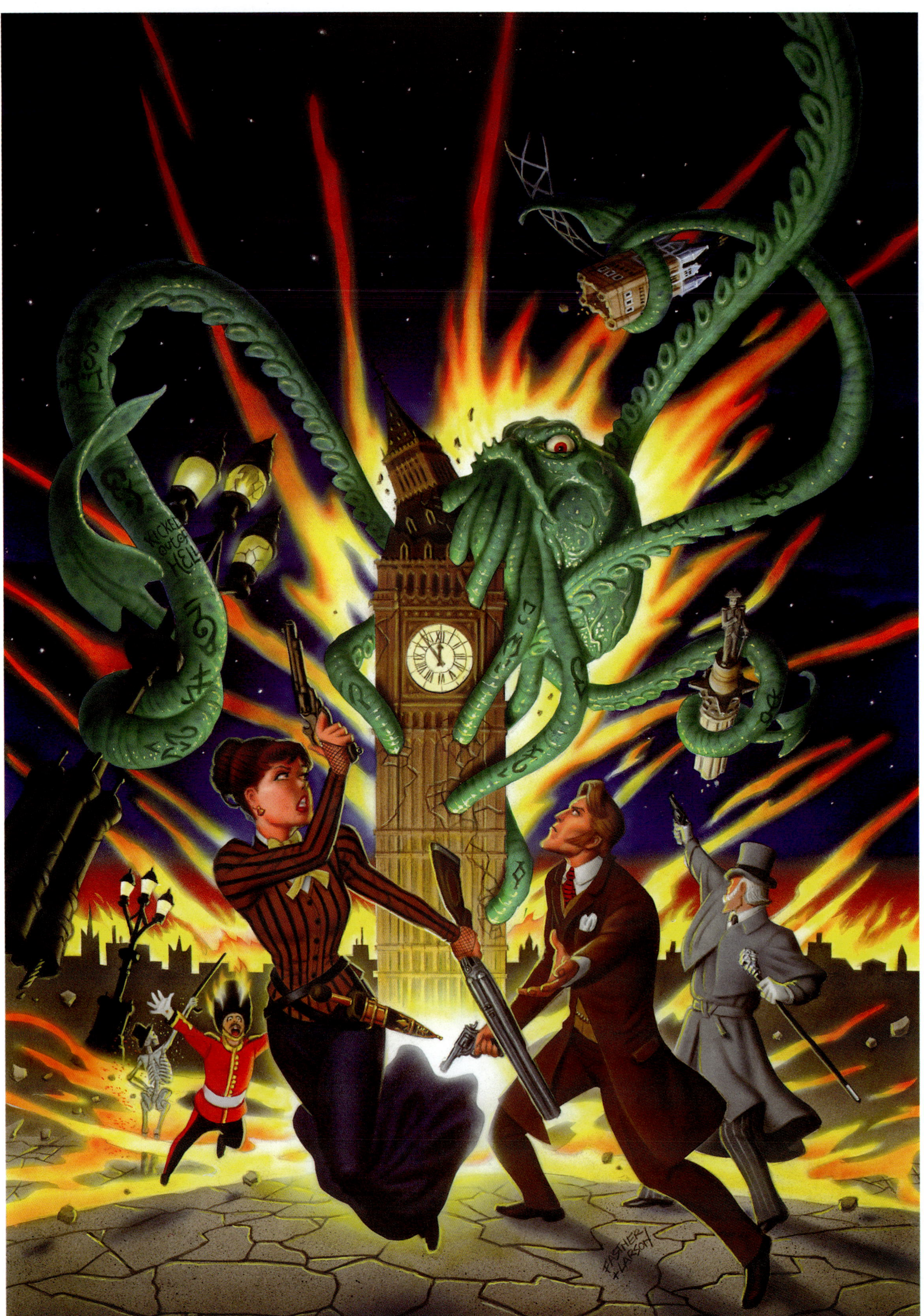

That Darned Squid God

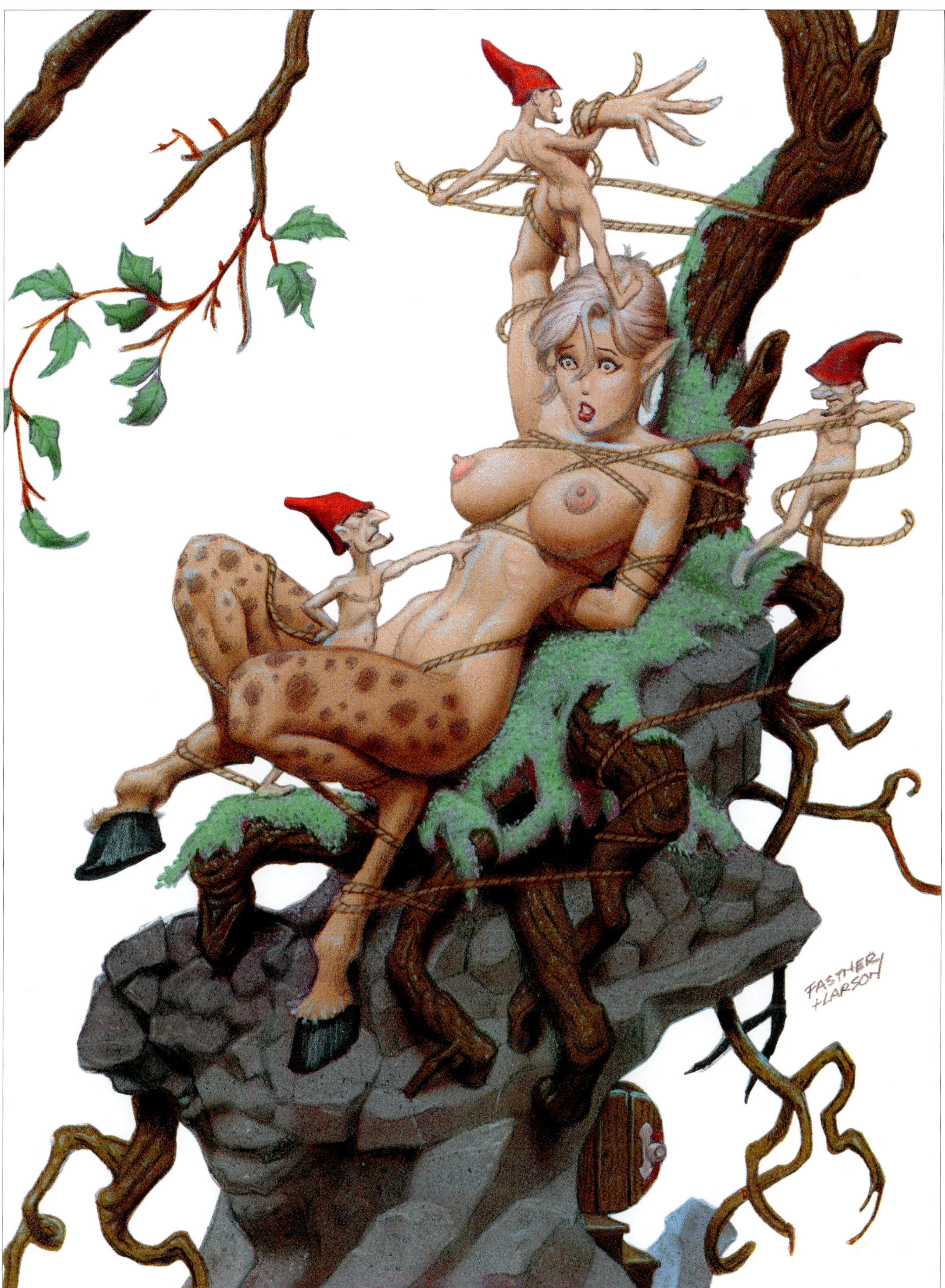

Wrong Place for a Nap

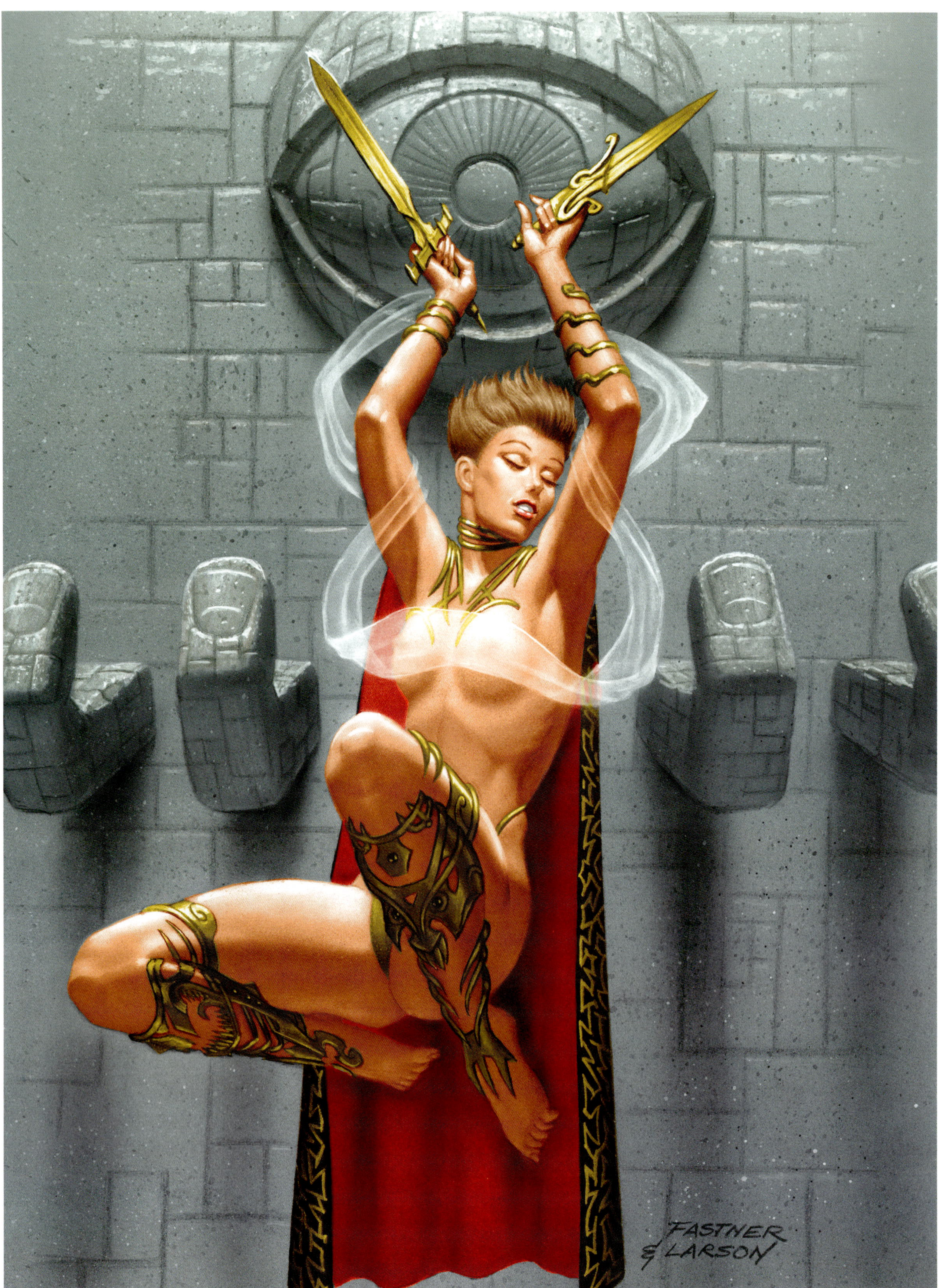

The All-Seeing

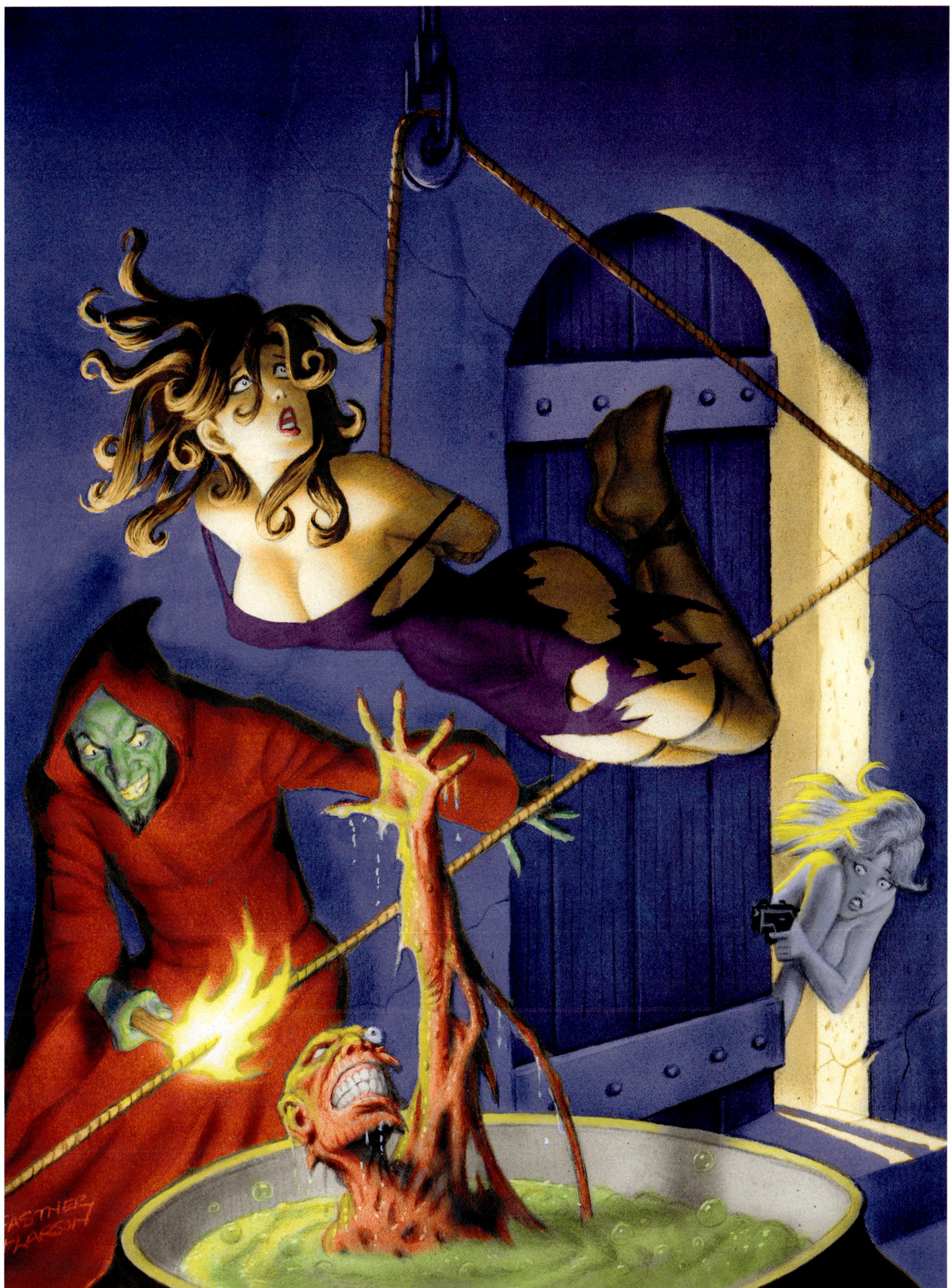

Vat of Evil

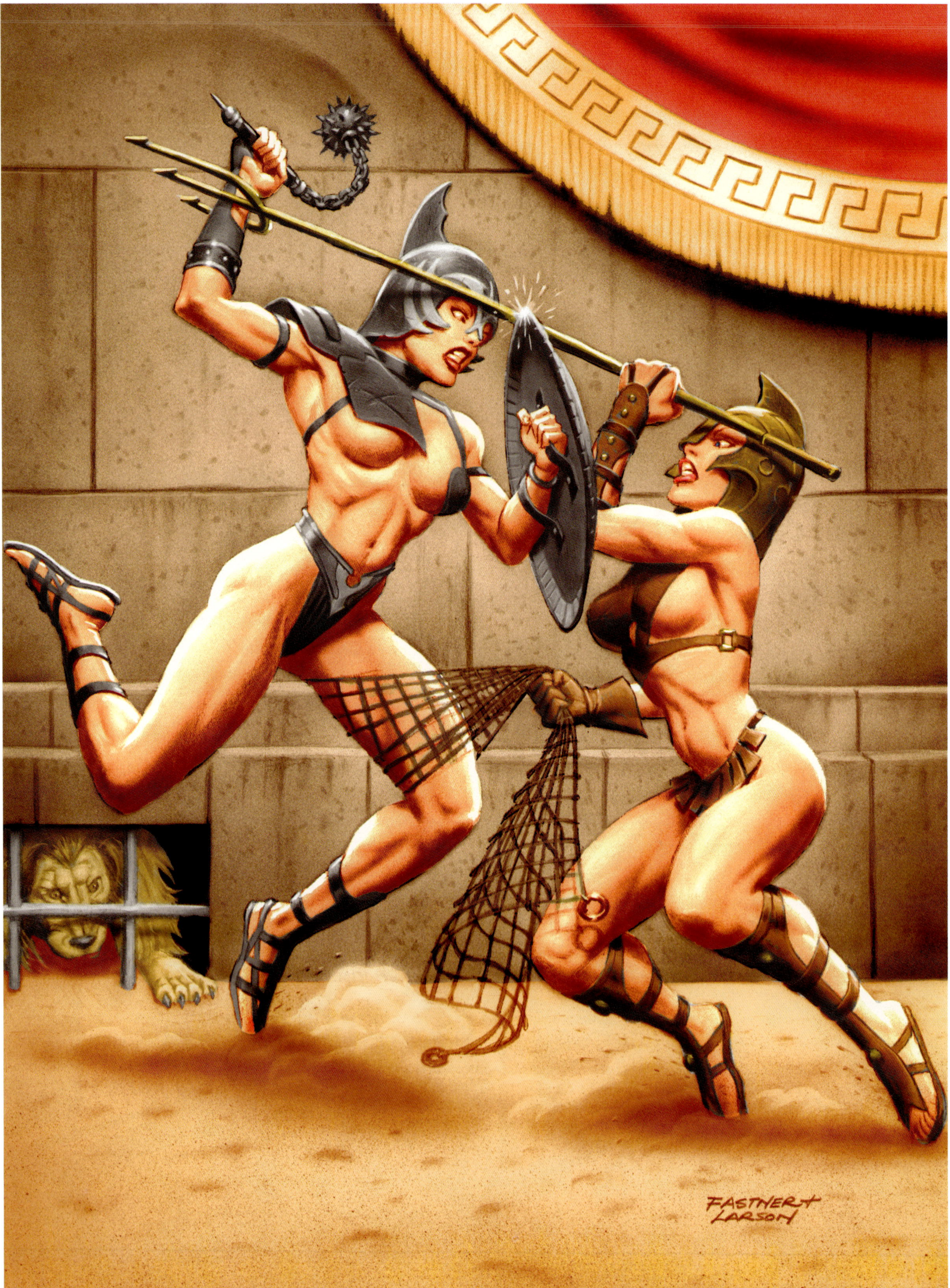

Gladiatrix

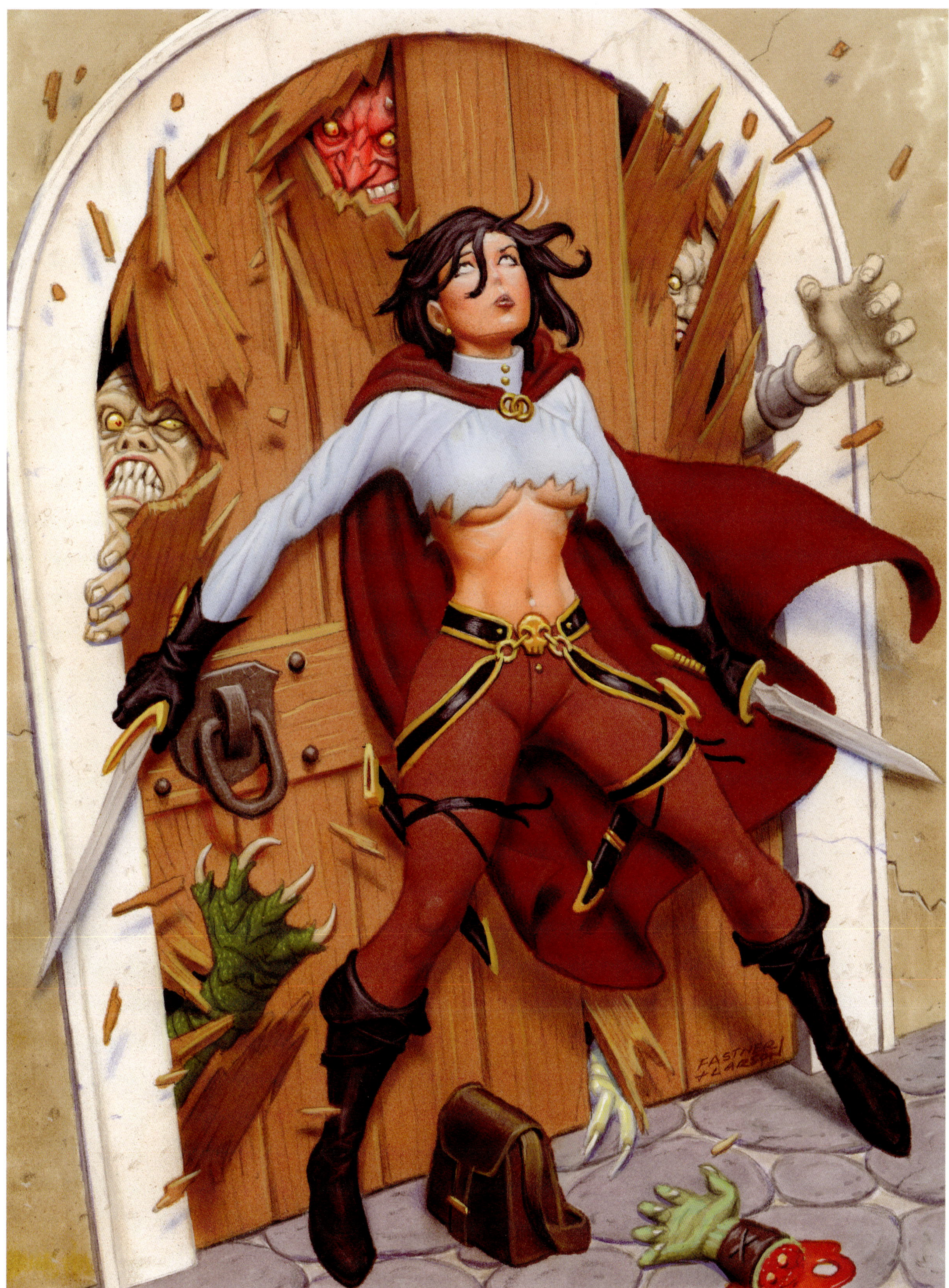

Gate Crashers

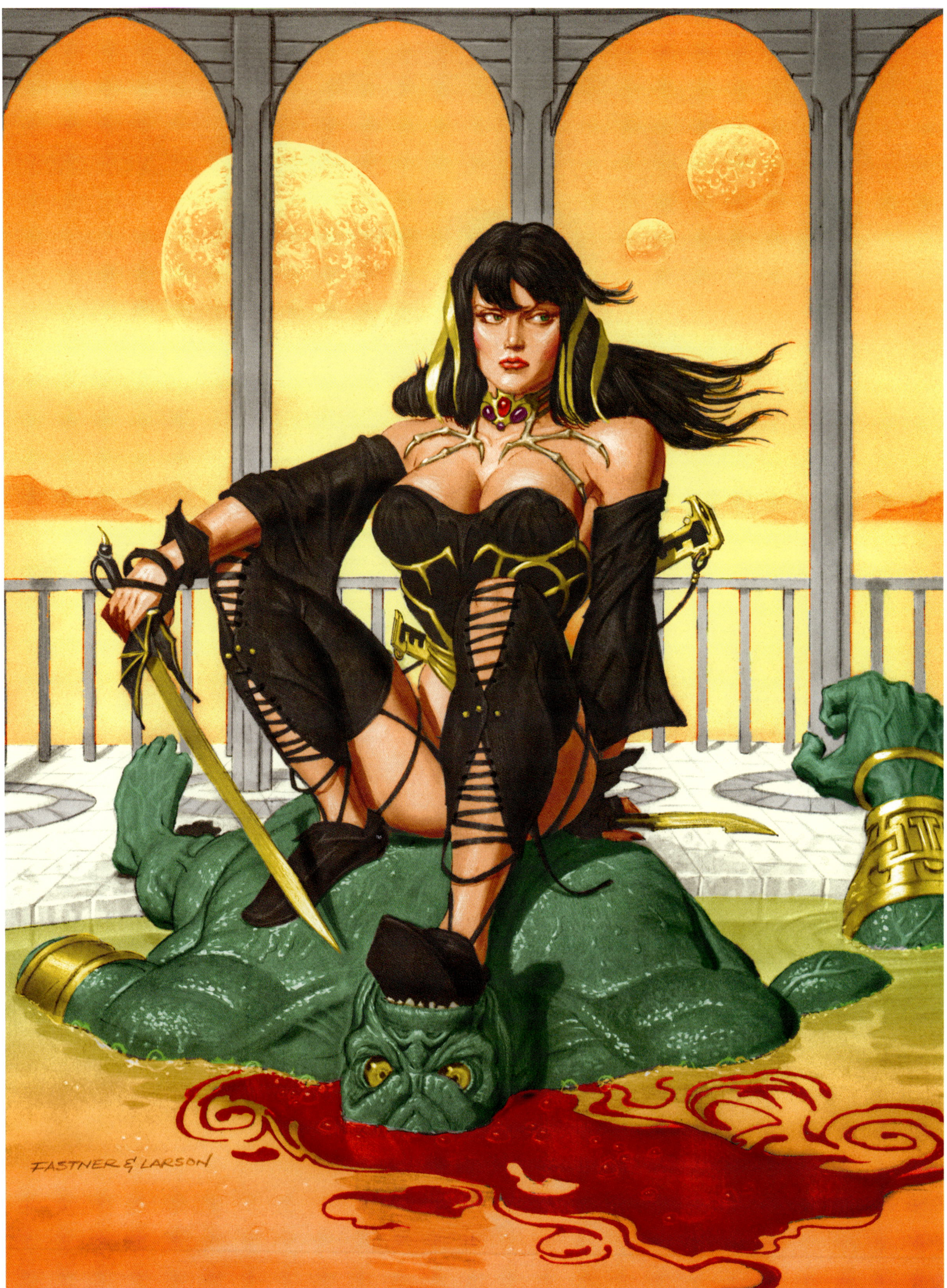

Moon Pool

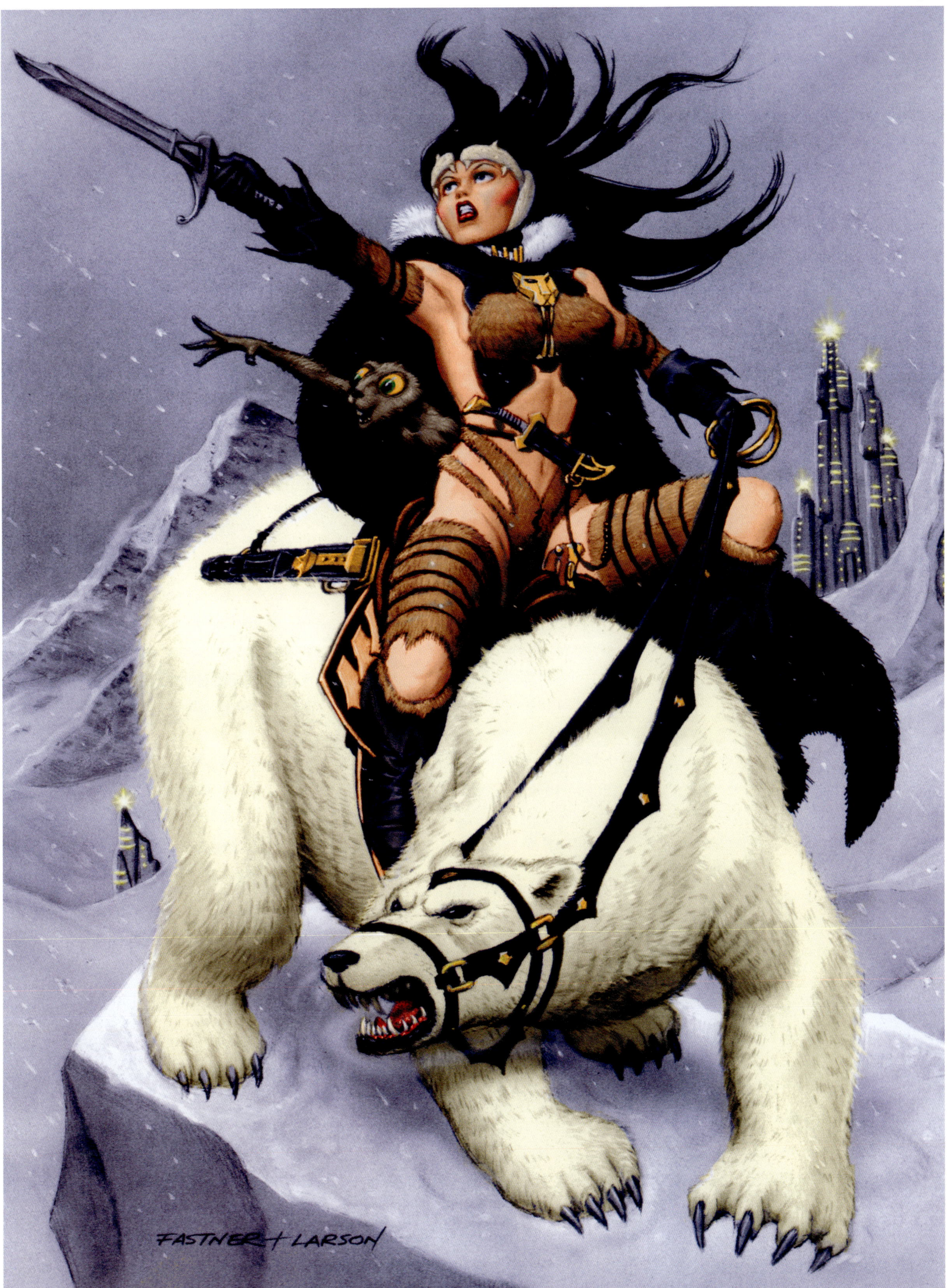

Ice Pals

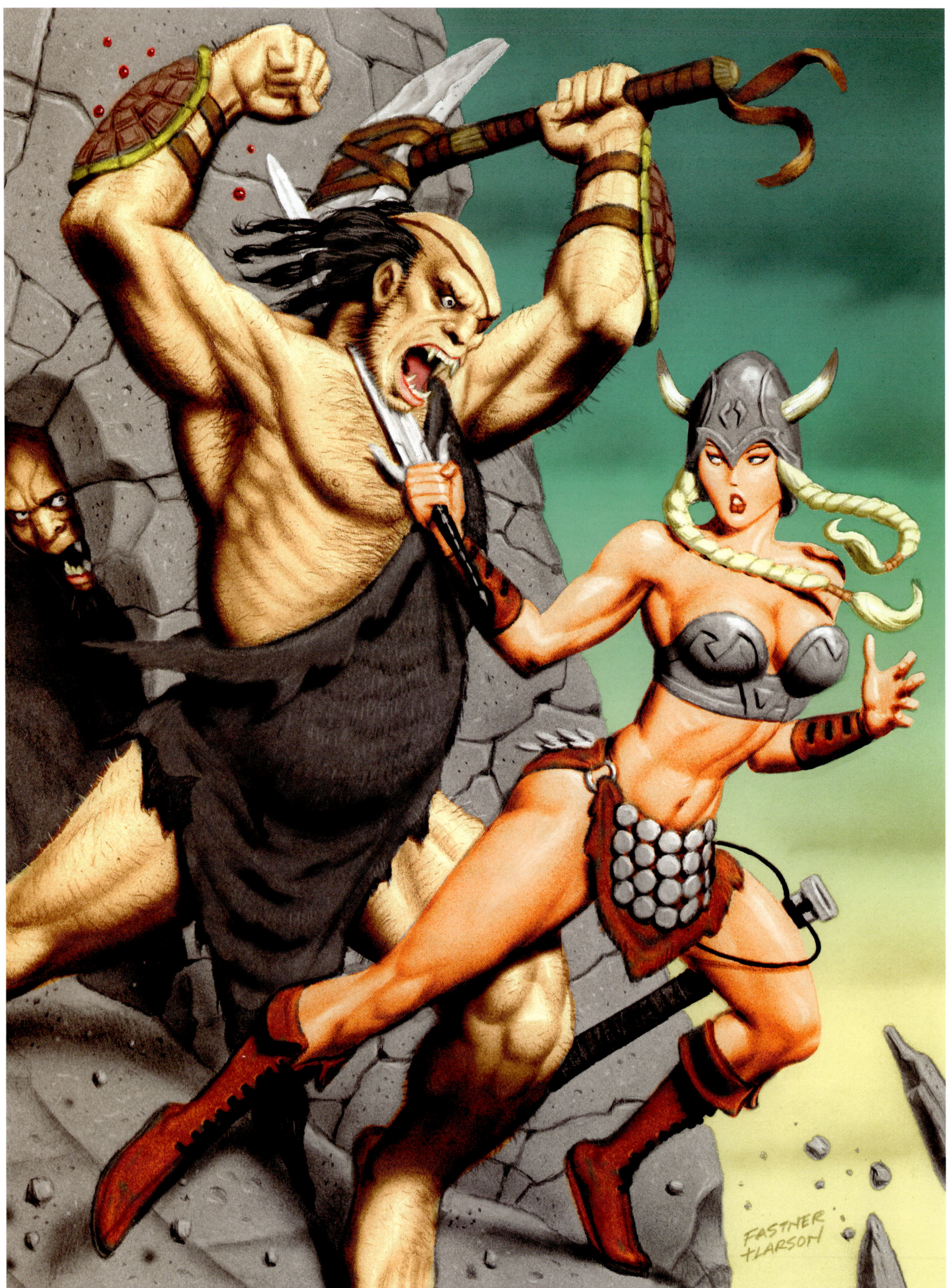

Ogg and Olga

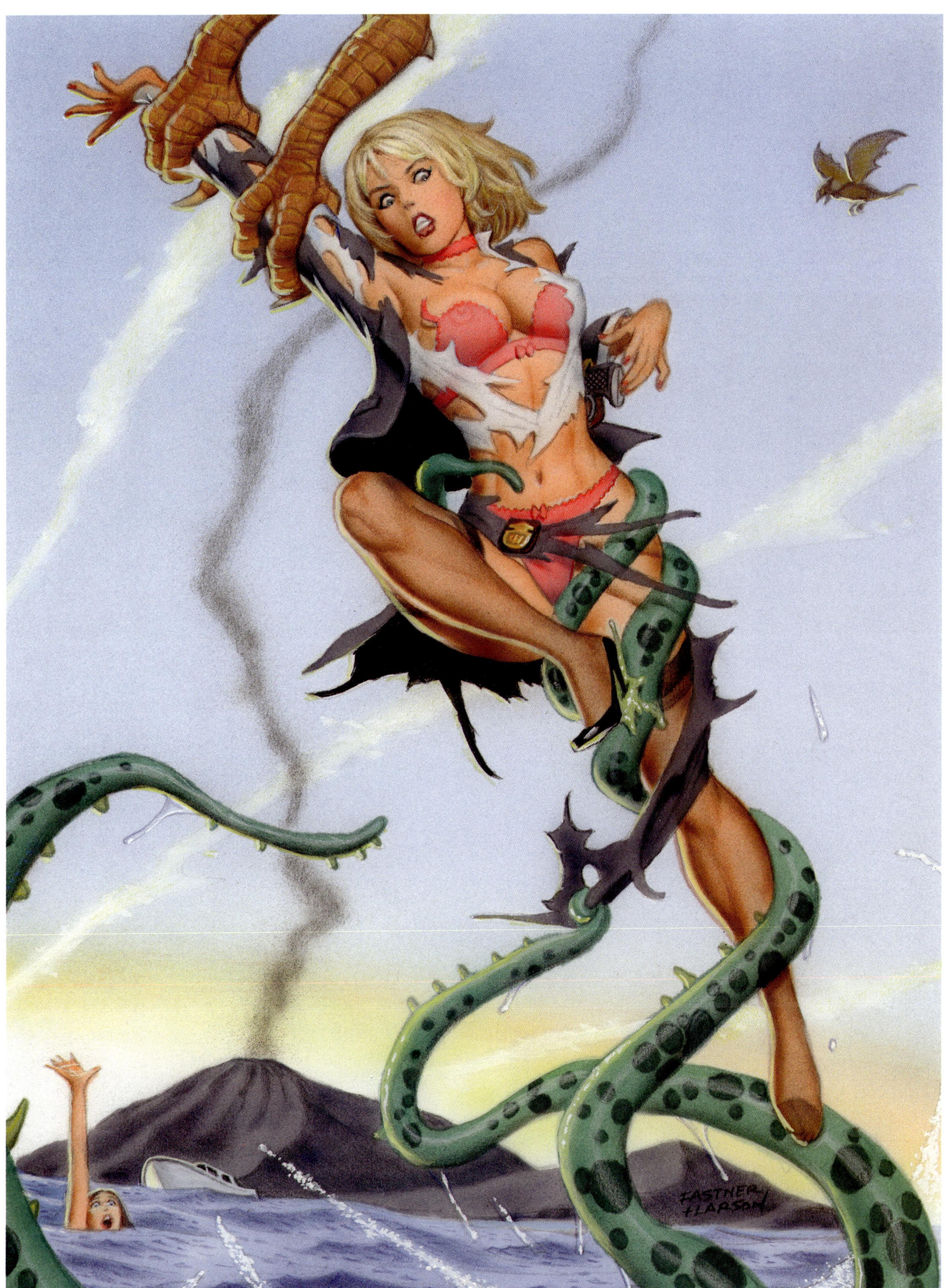

Double Trouble

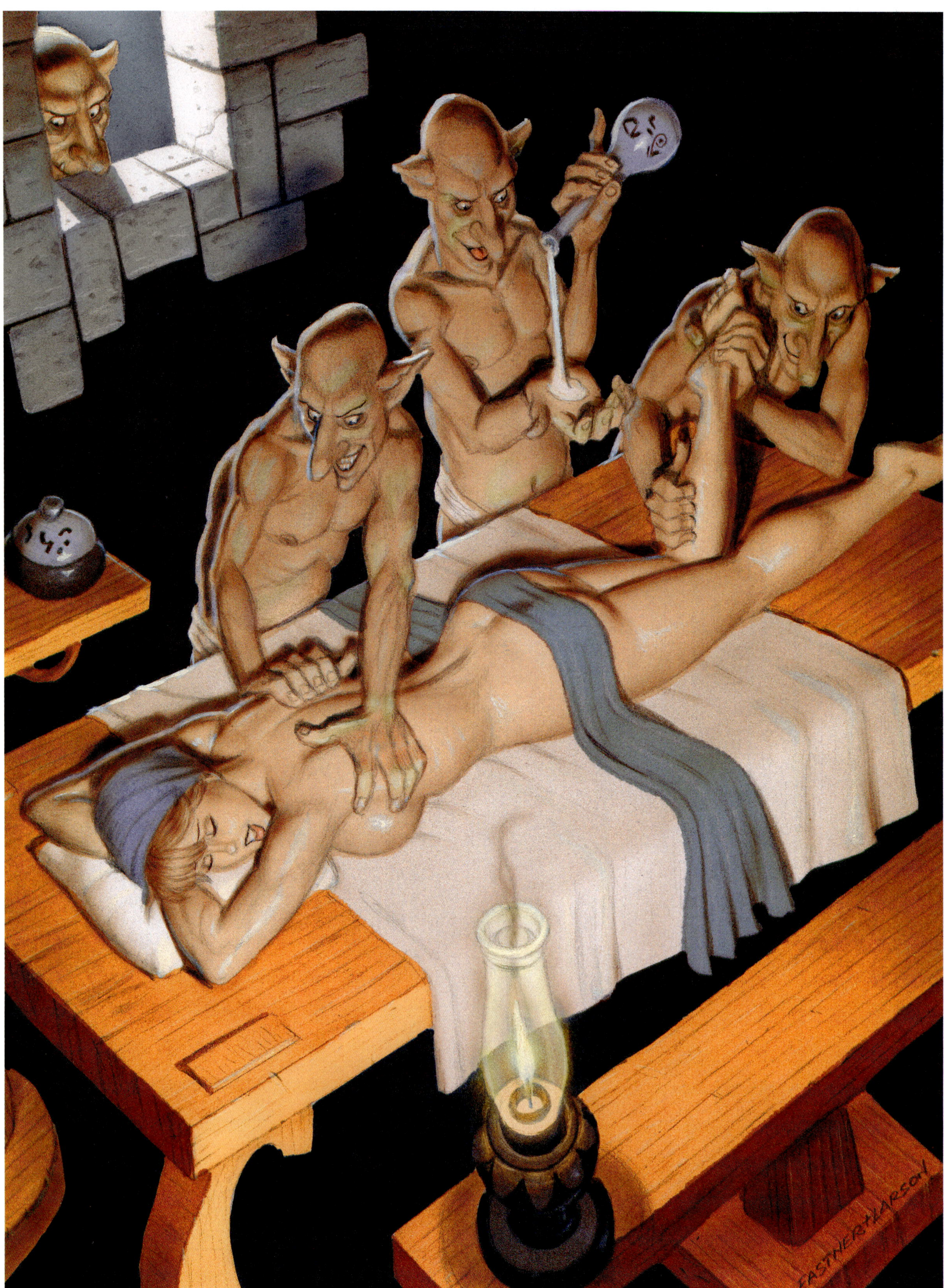

Troll Rubdown

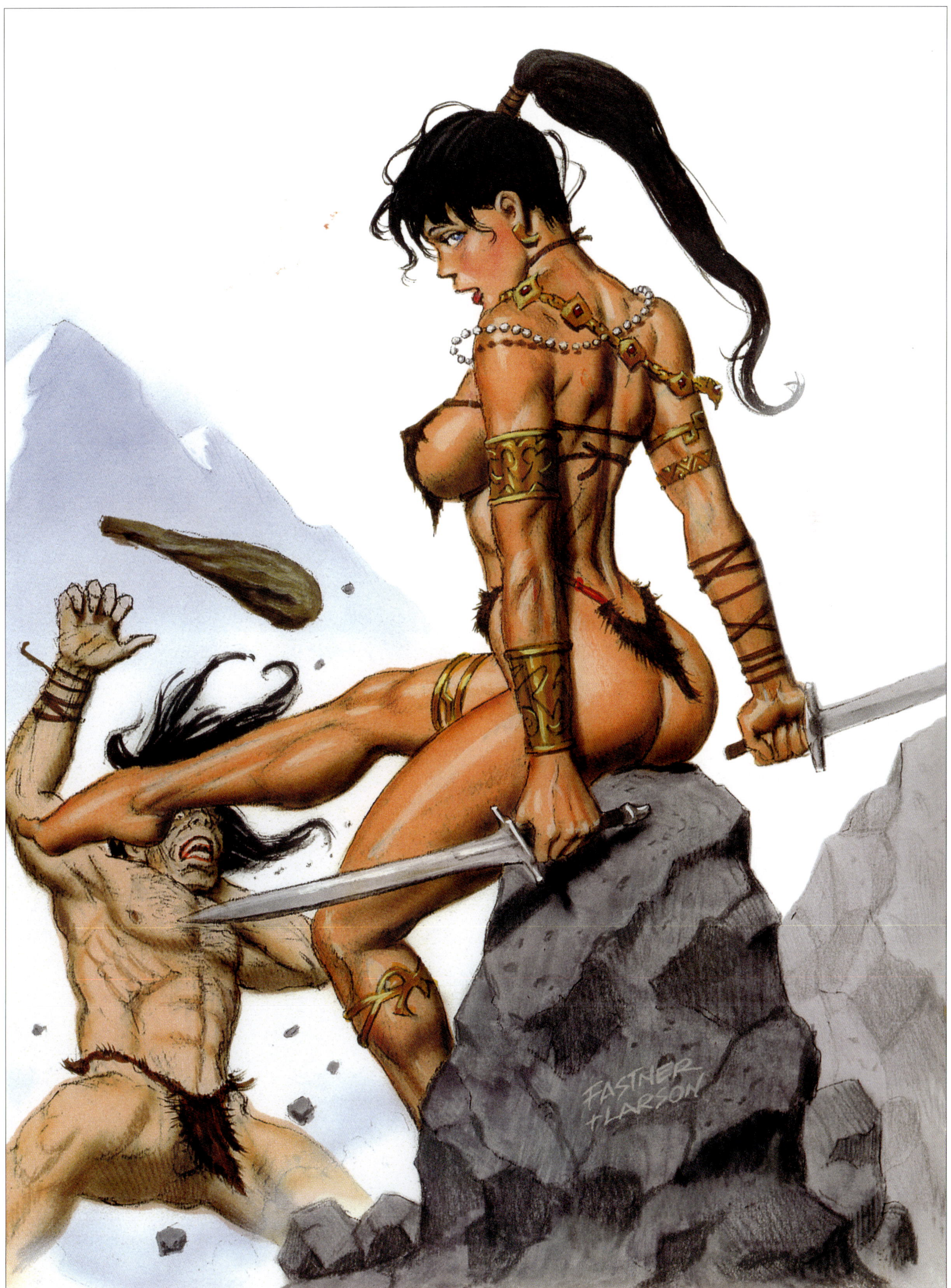

This Seat's Taken

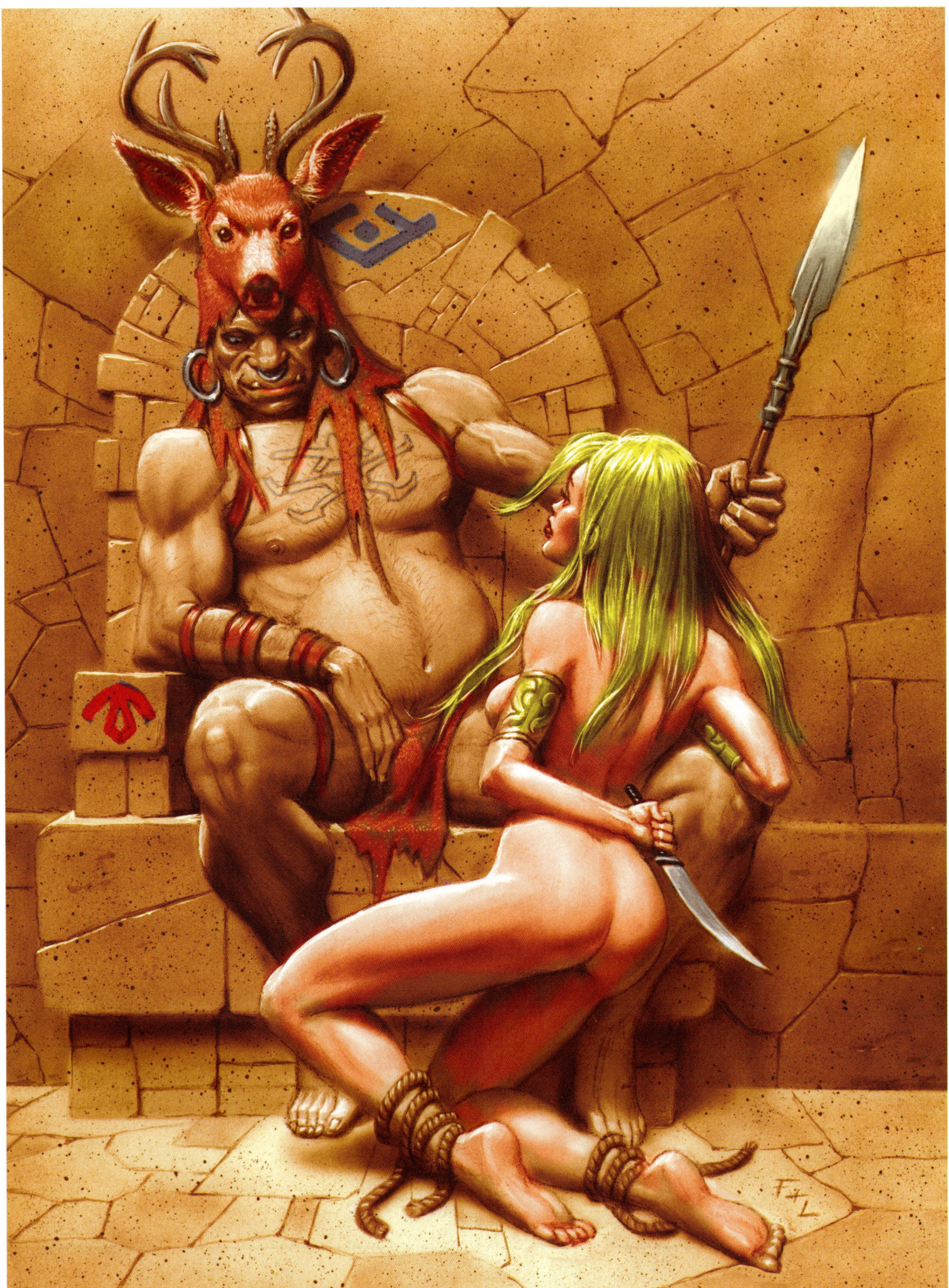

Assassin

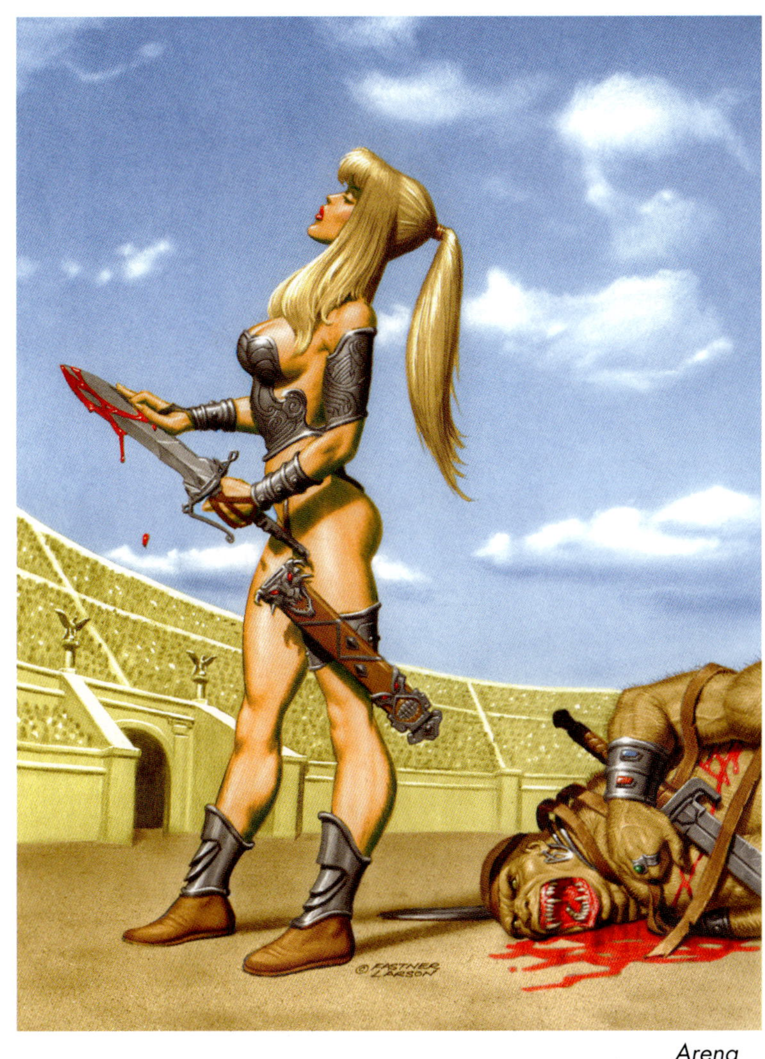

Arena

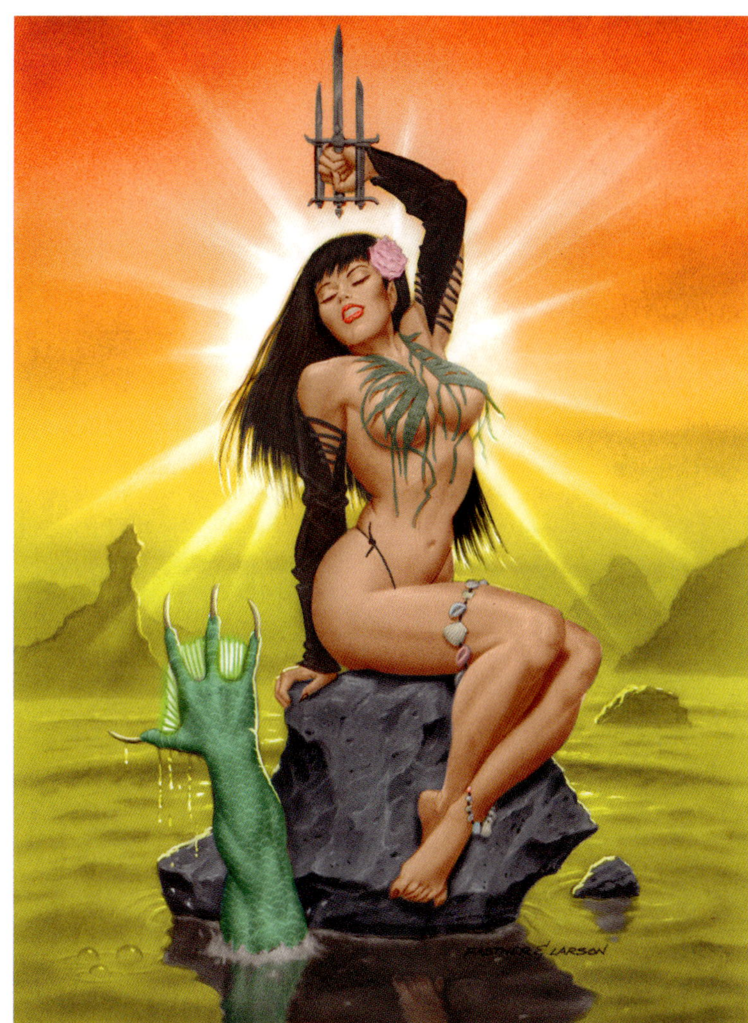

Siren Song

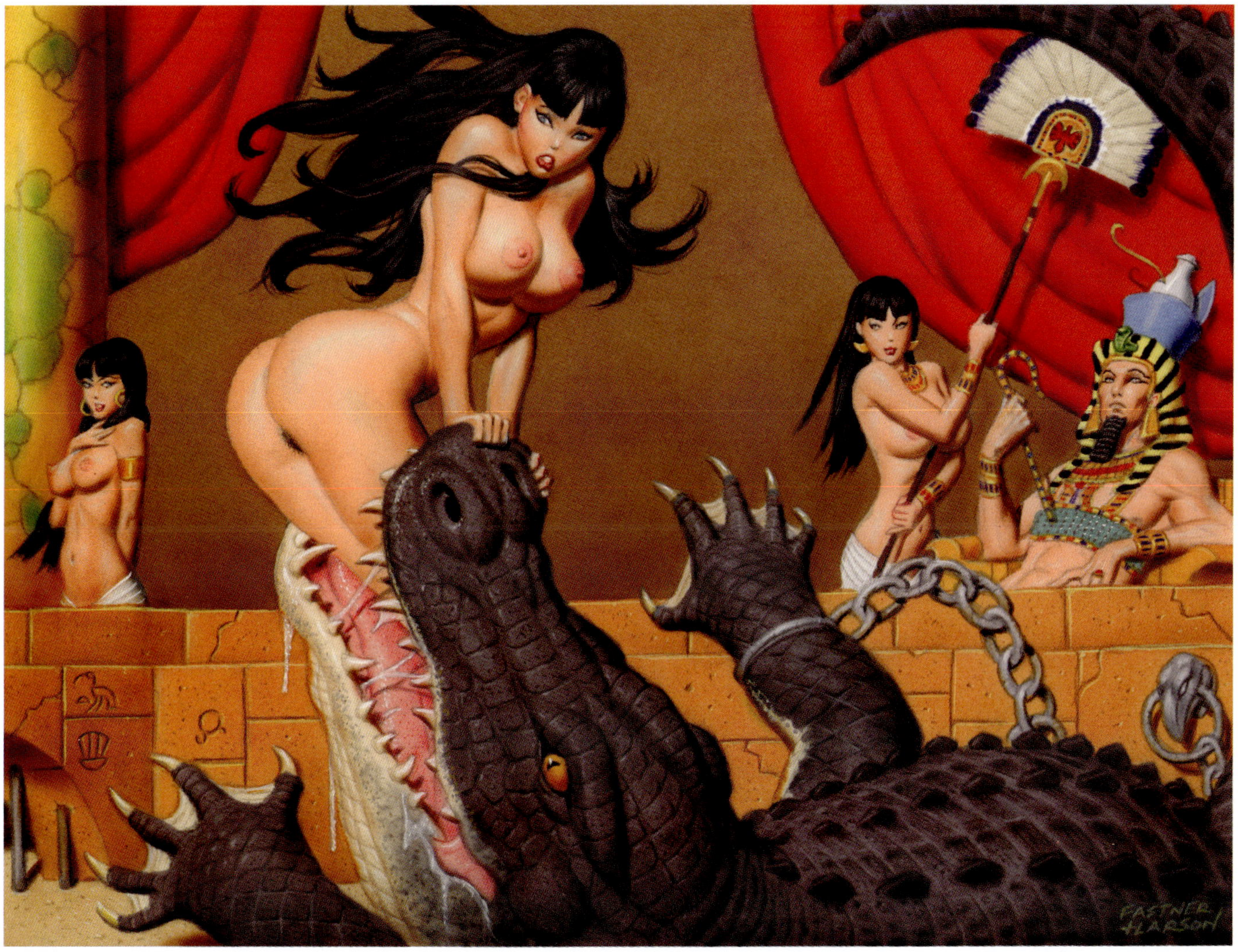

Fallen From Favor

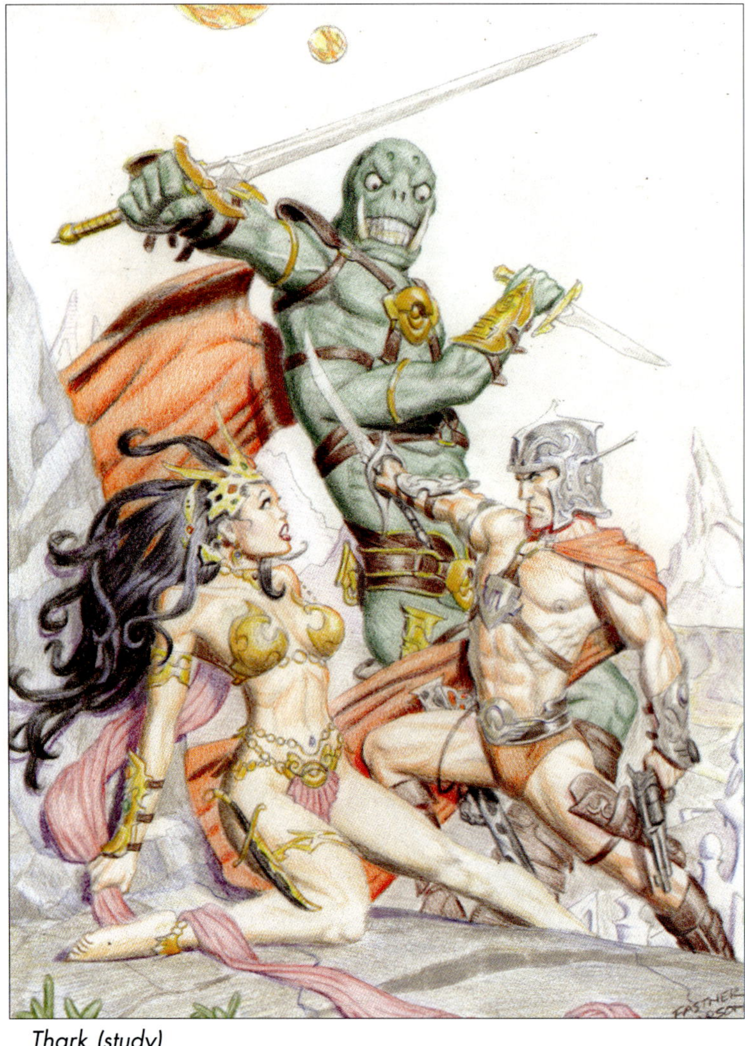

Thark (study)

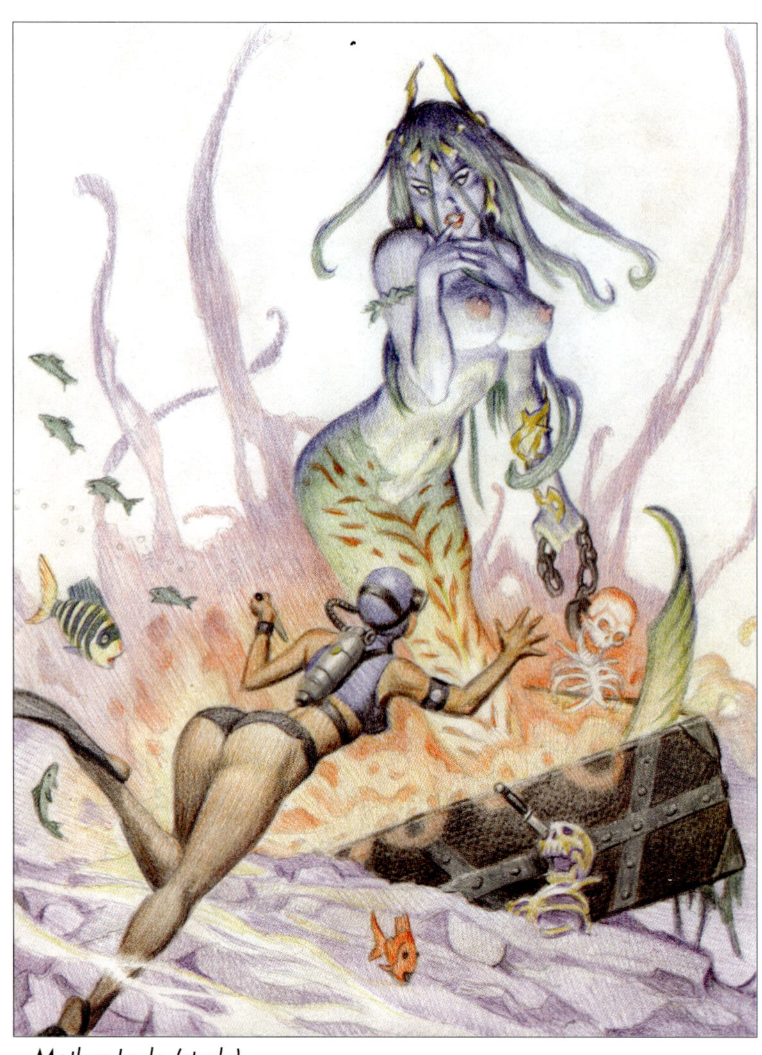

Mother Lode (study)

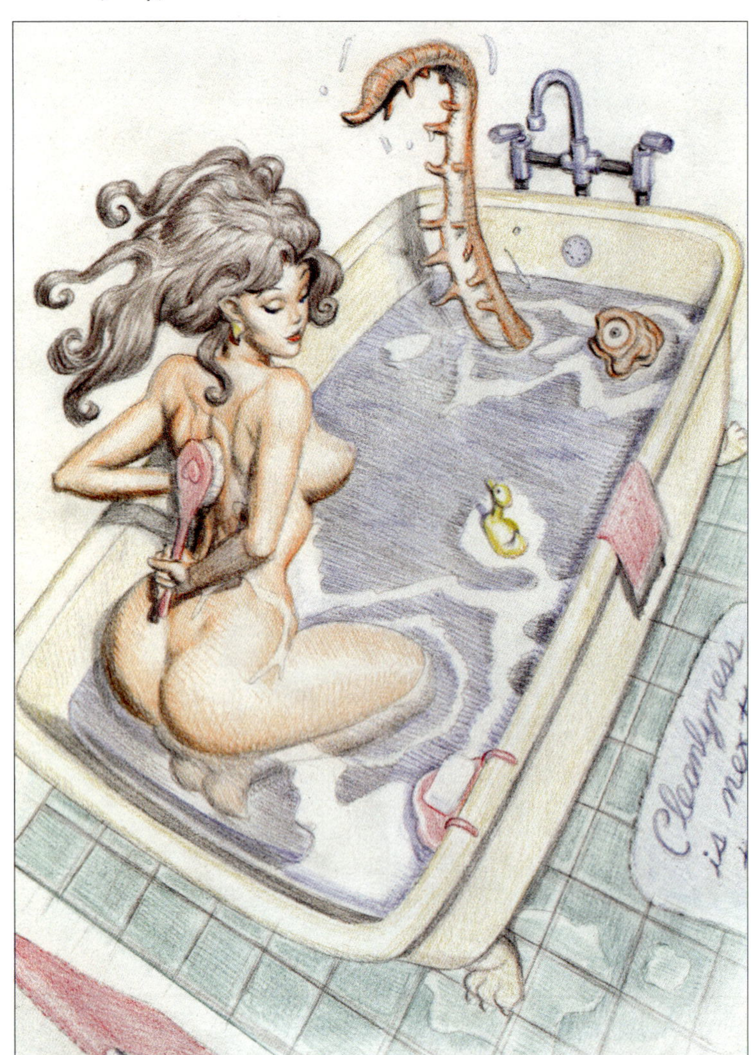

Clawfoot Tub (study)

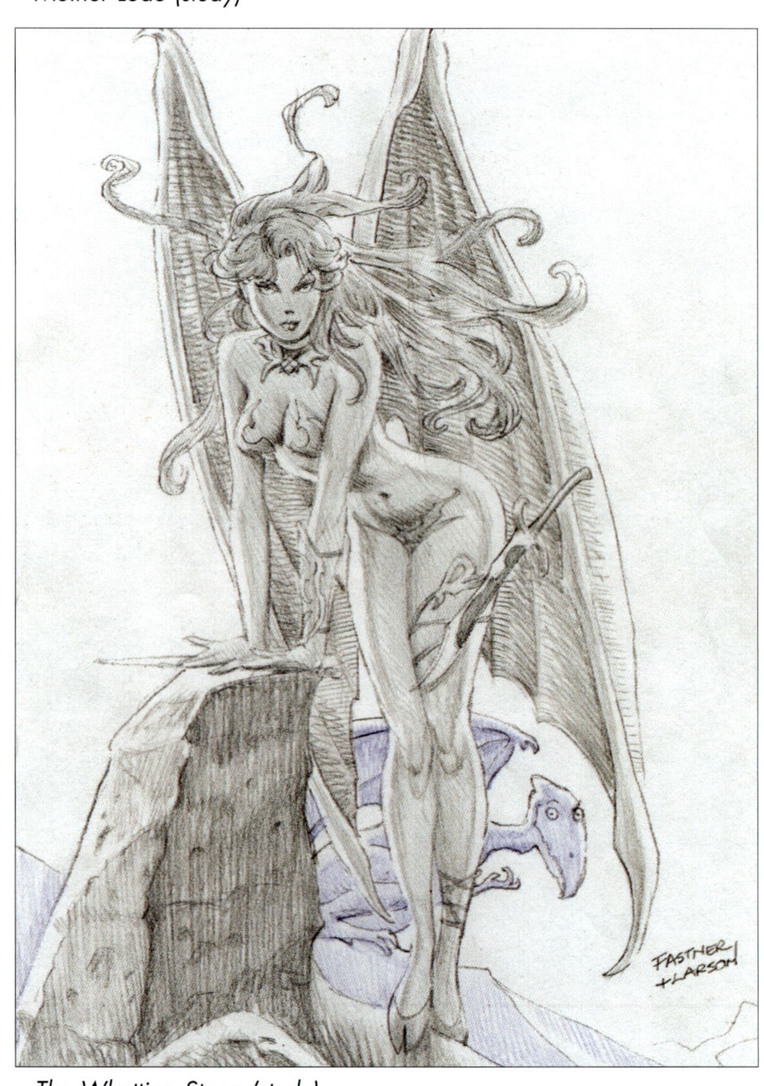

The Whetting Stone (study)

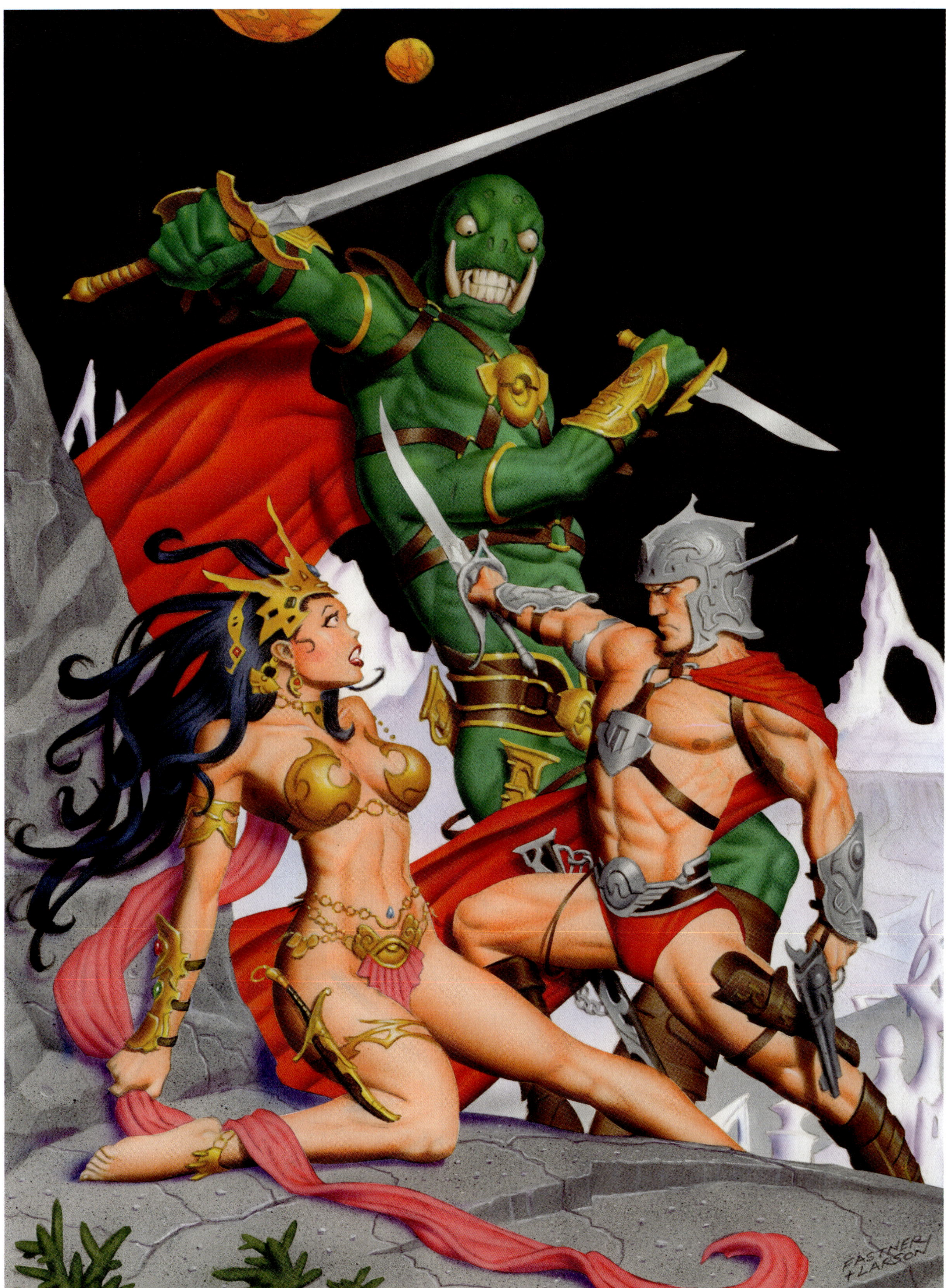

Thark (painting)

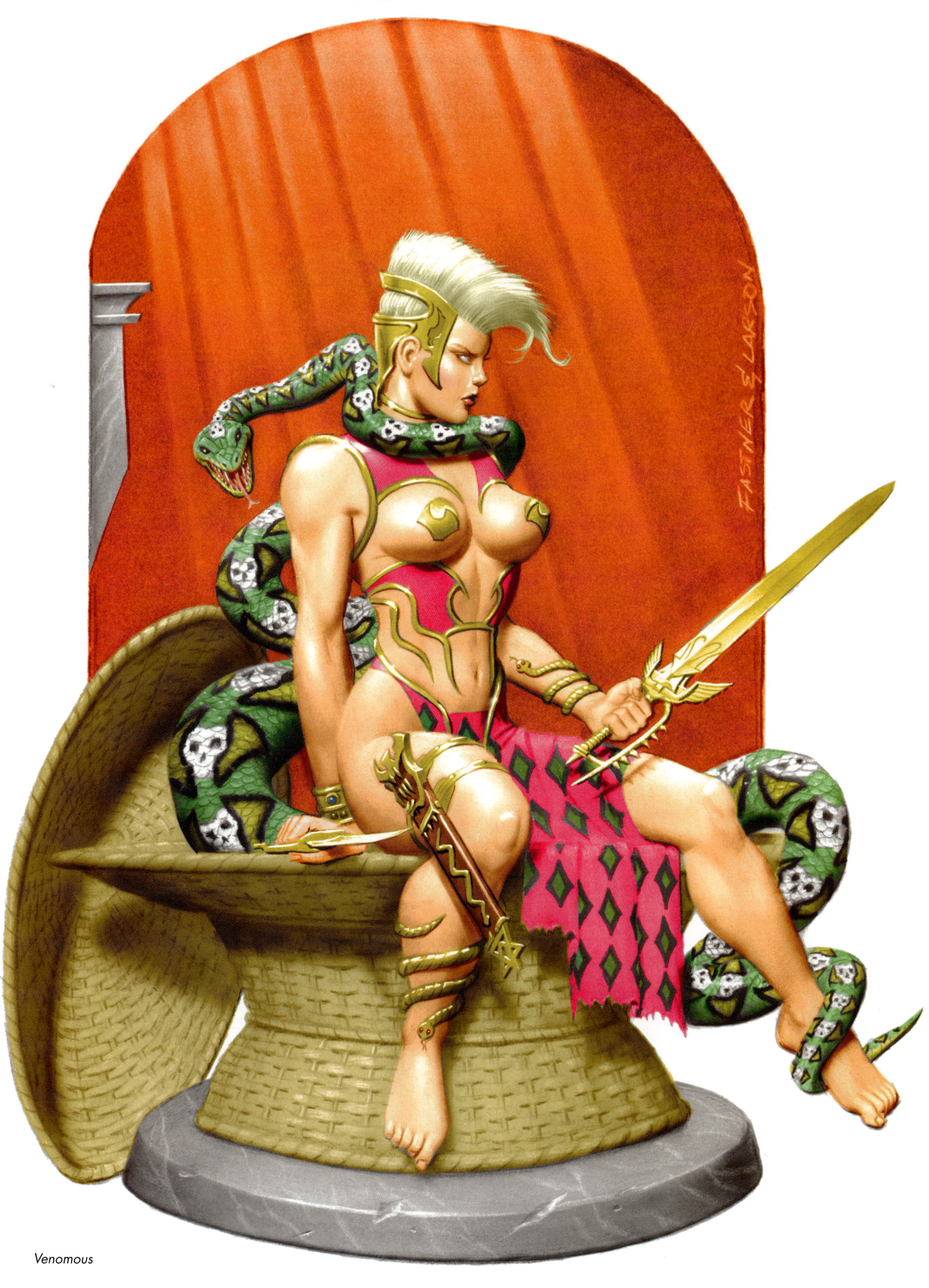

Venomous

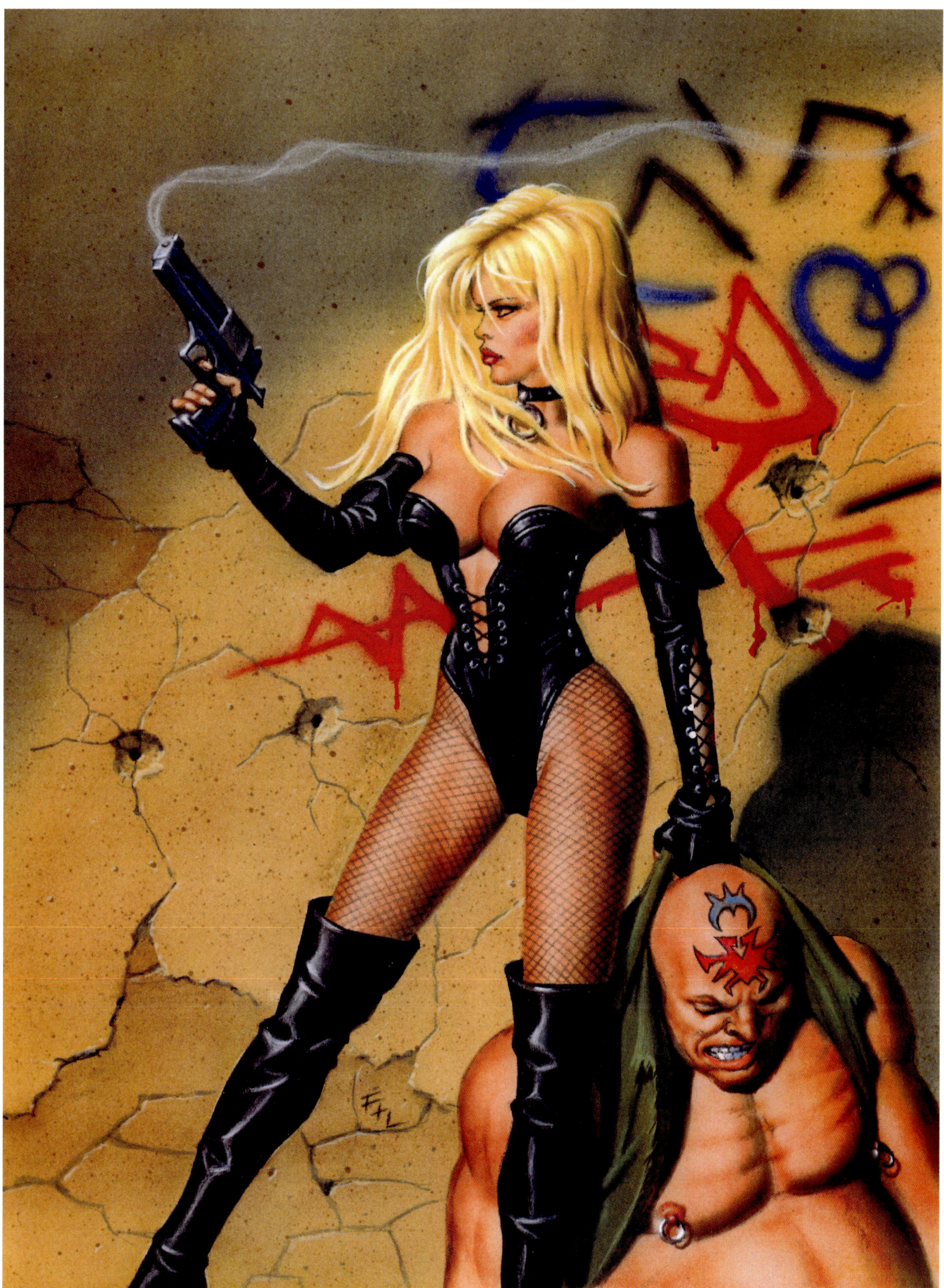

Hotwired

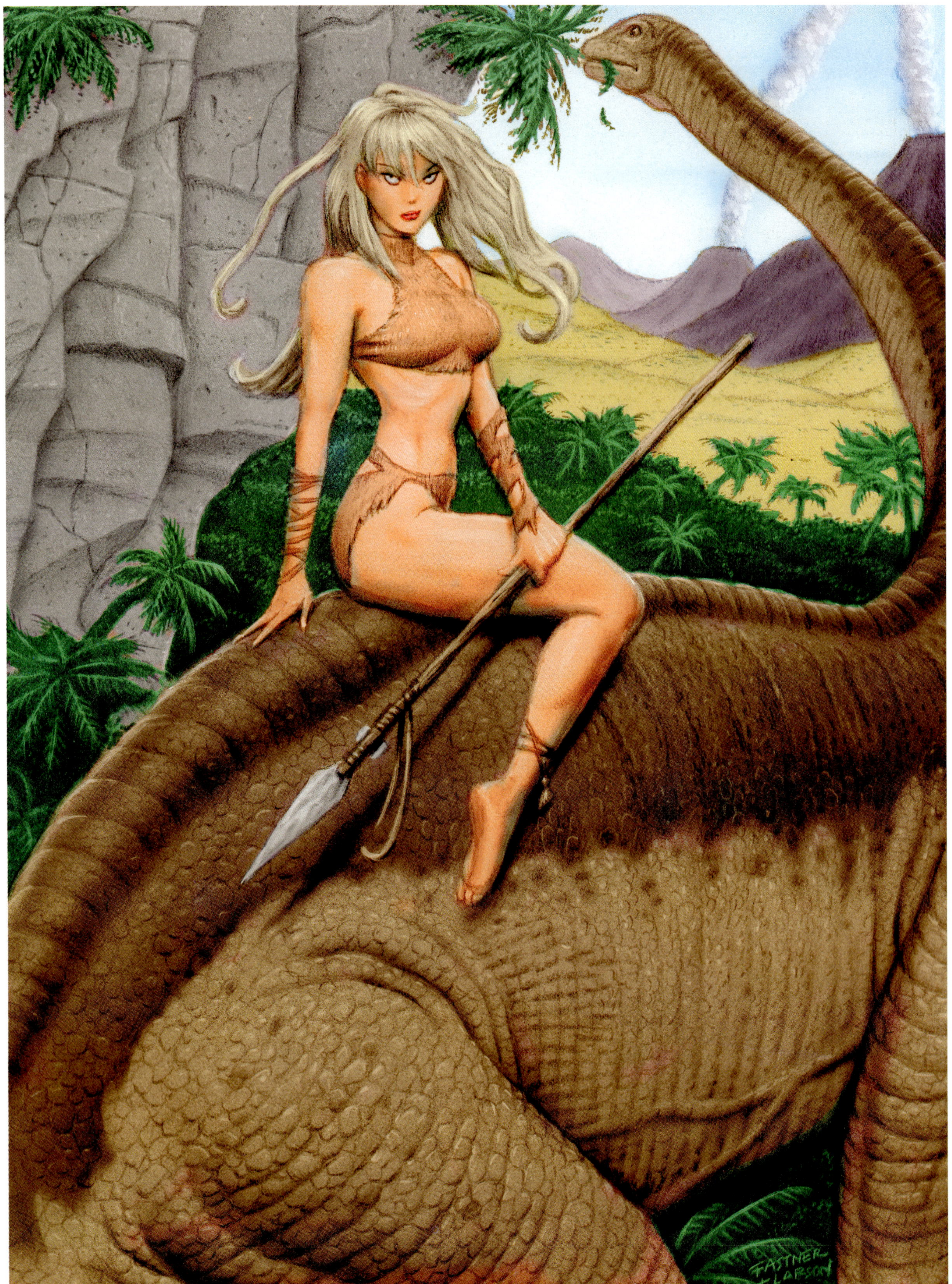

Apatosaur

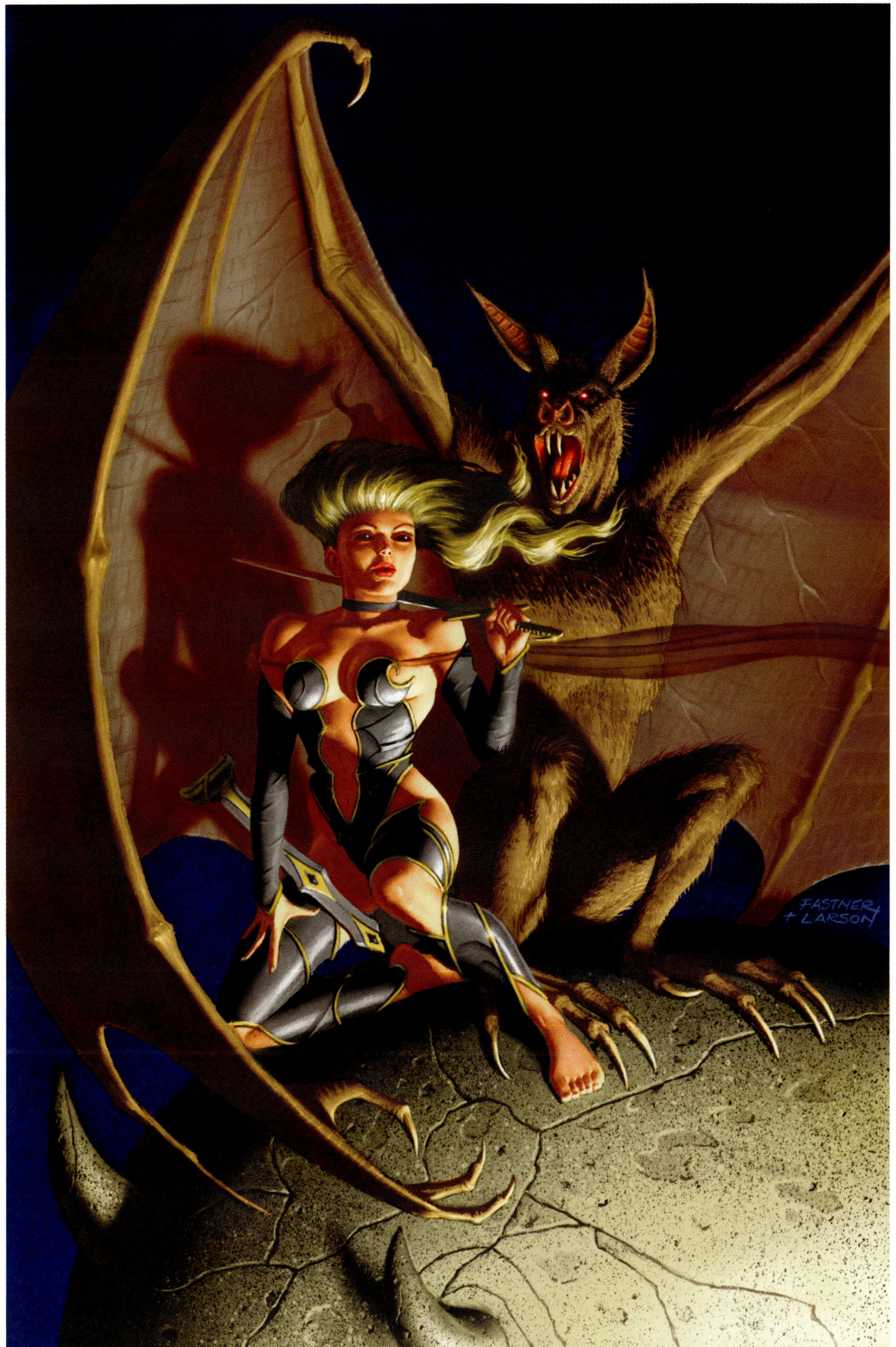

Night Slayers

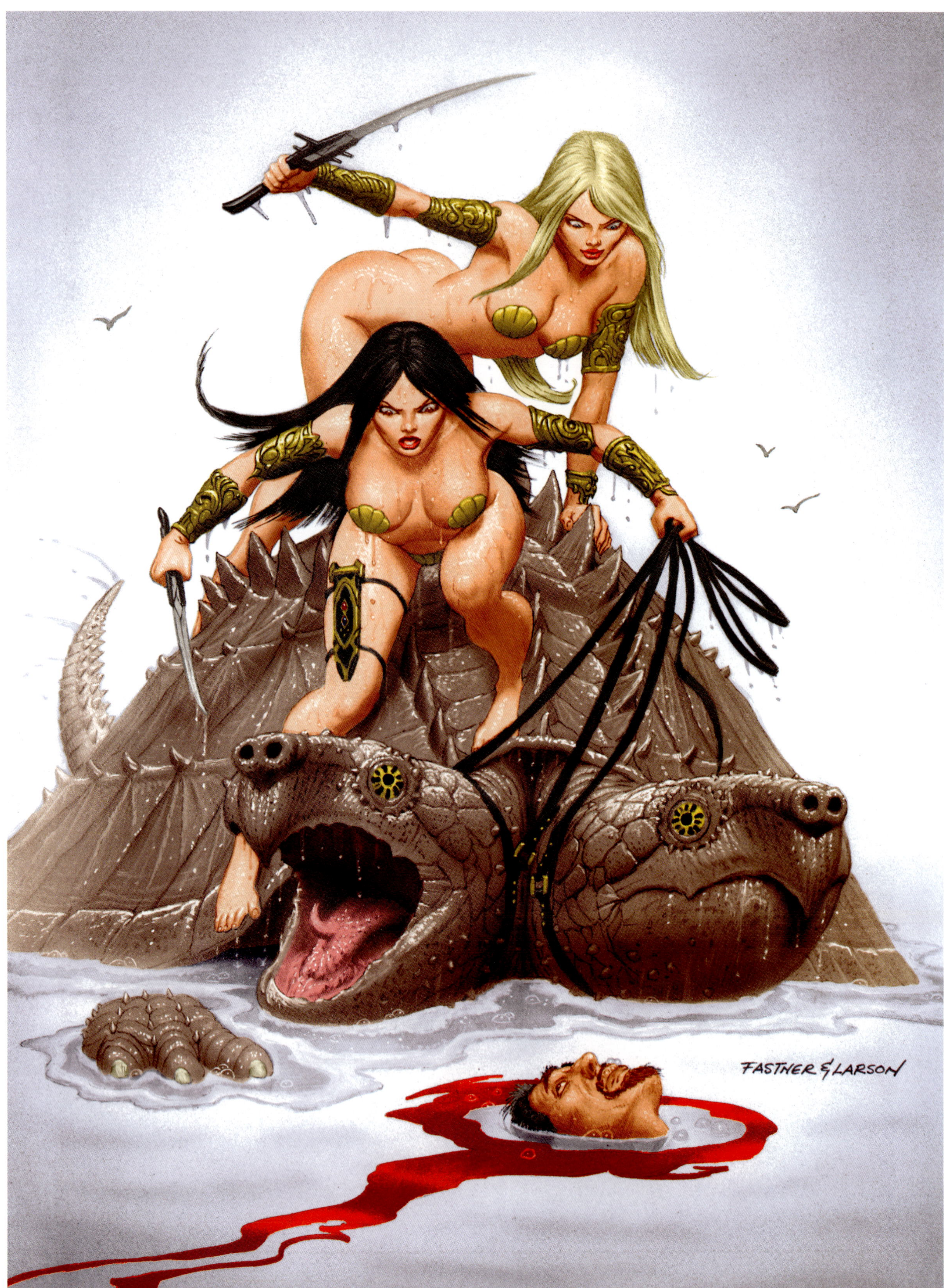

Snappers

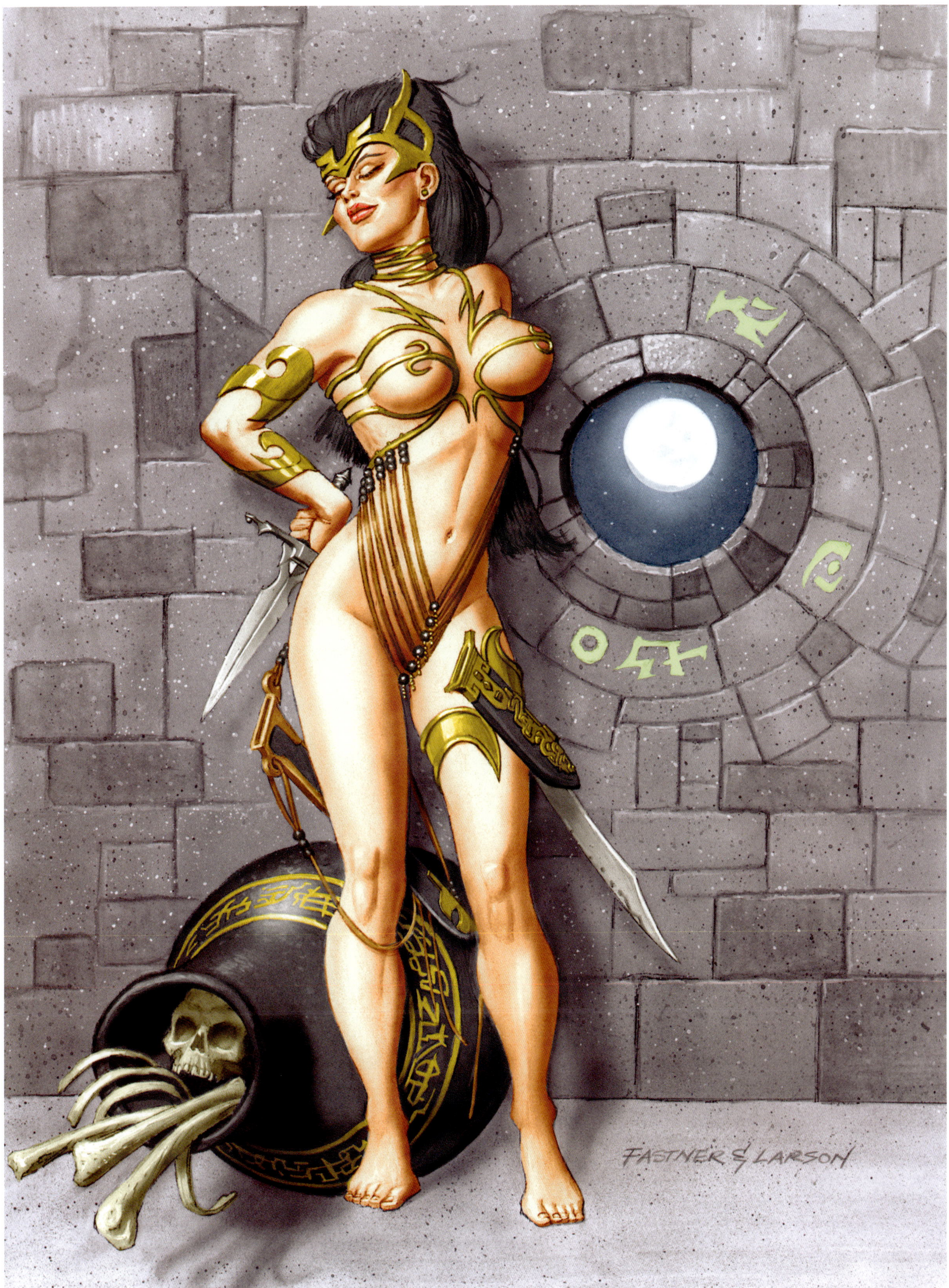

Unurned

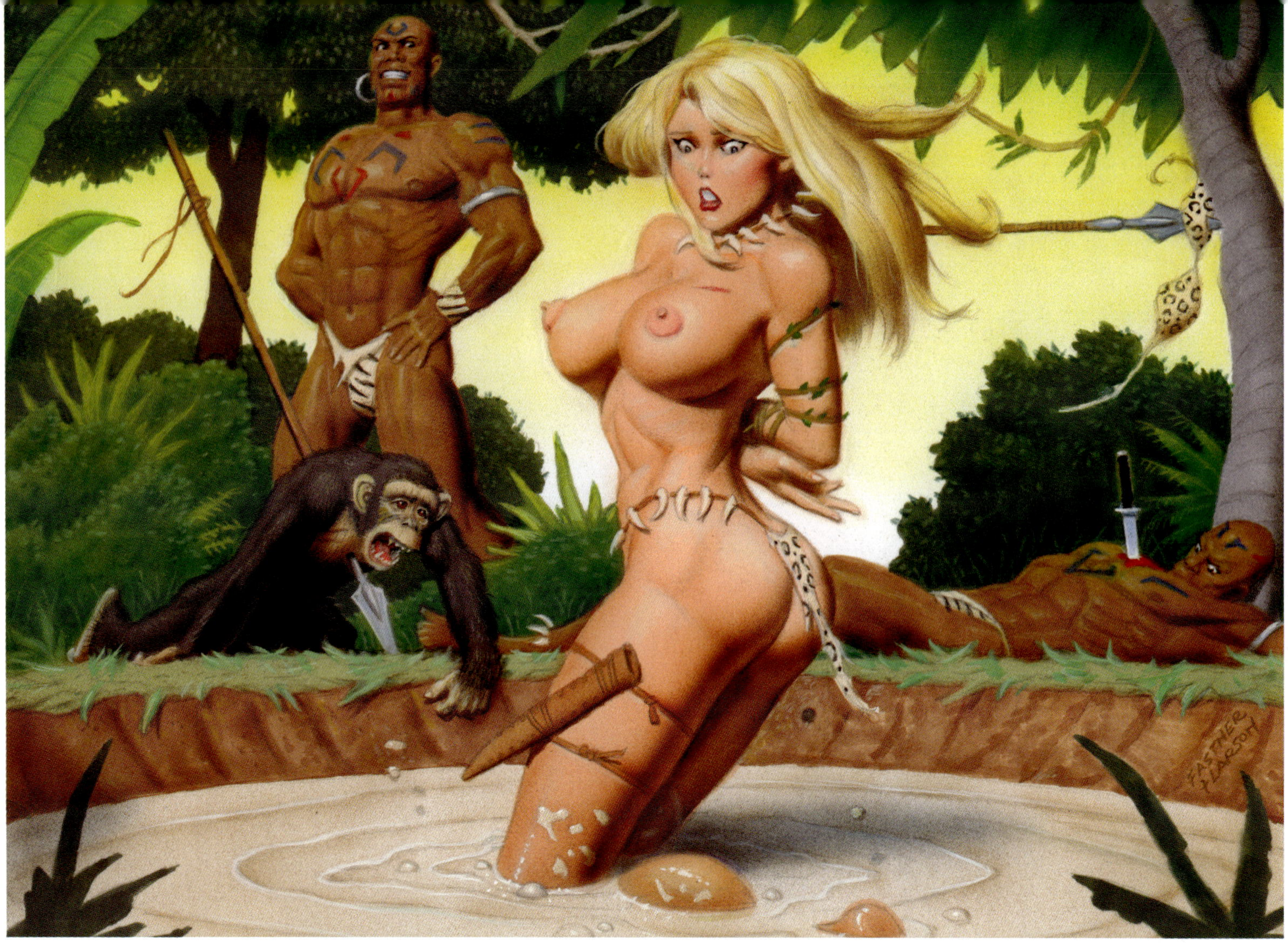

That Sinking Feeling

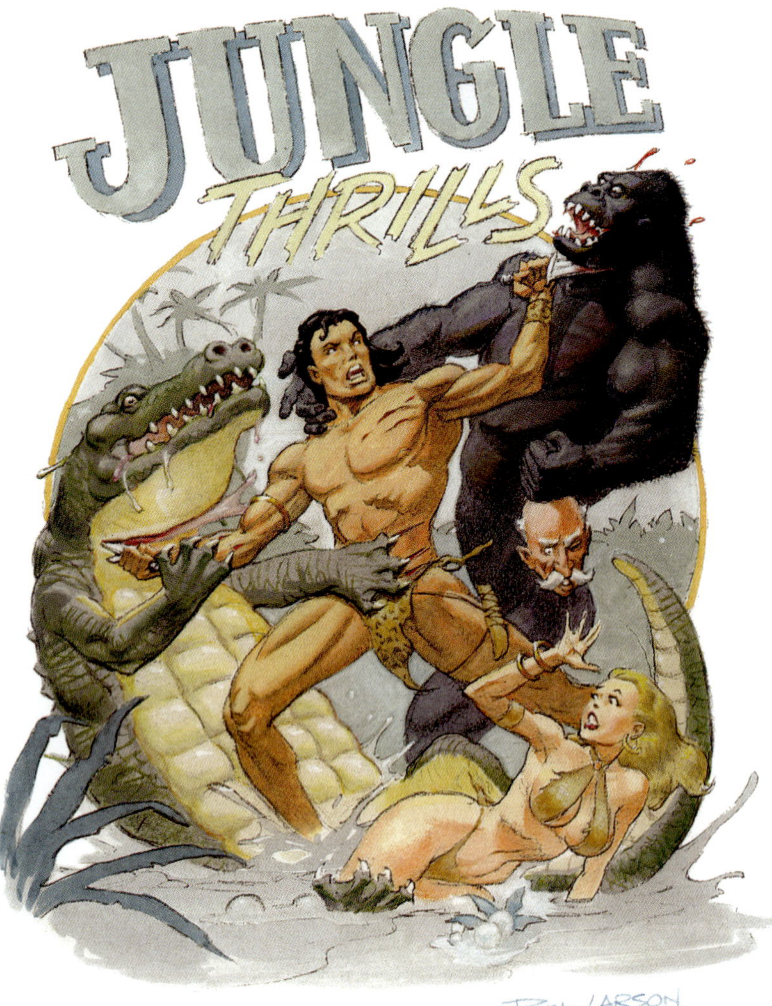

Jungle Thrills

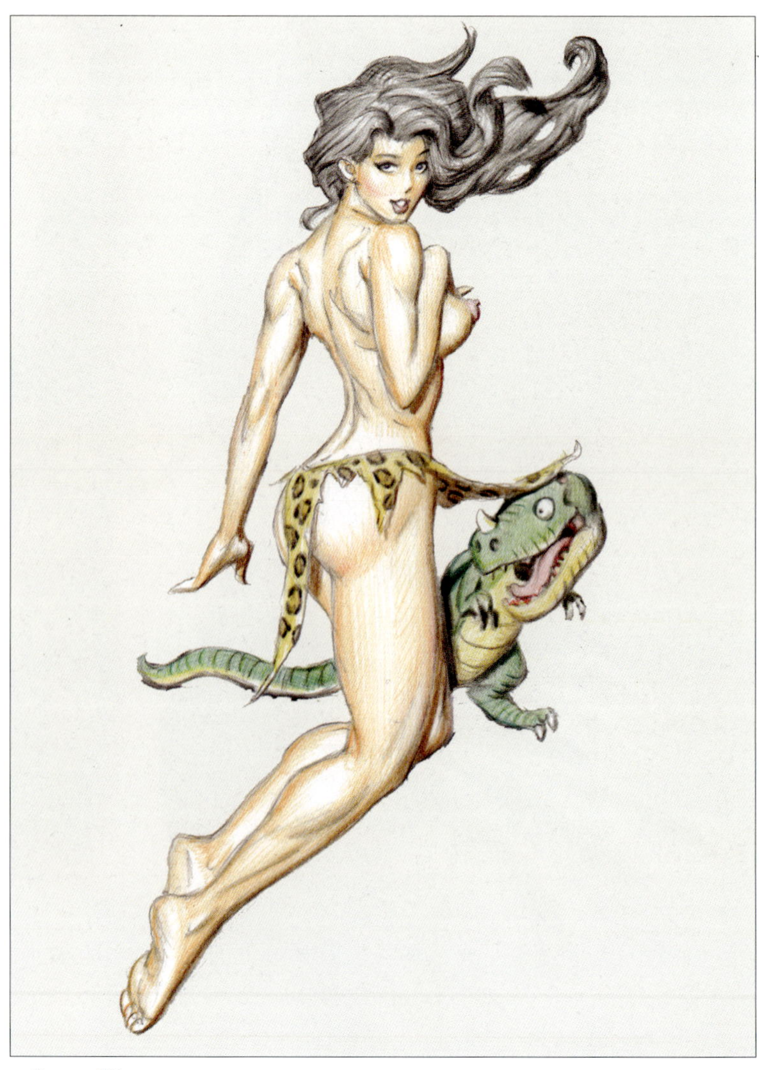

Pervy Dino

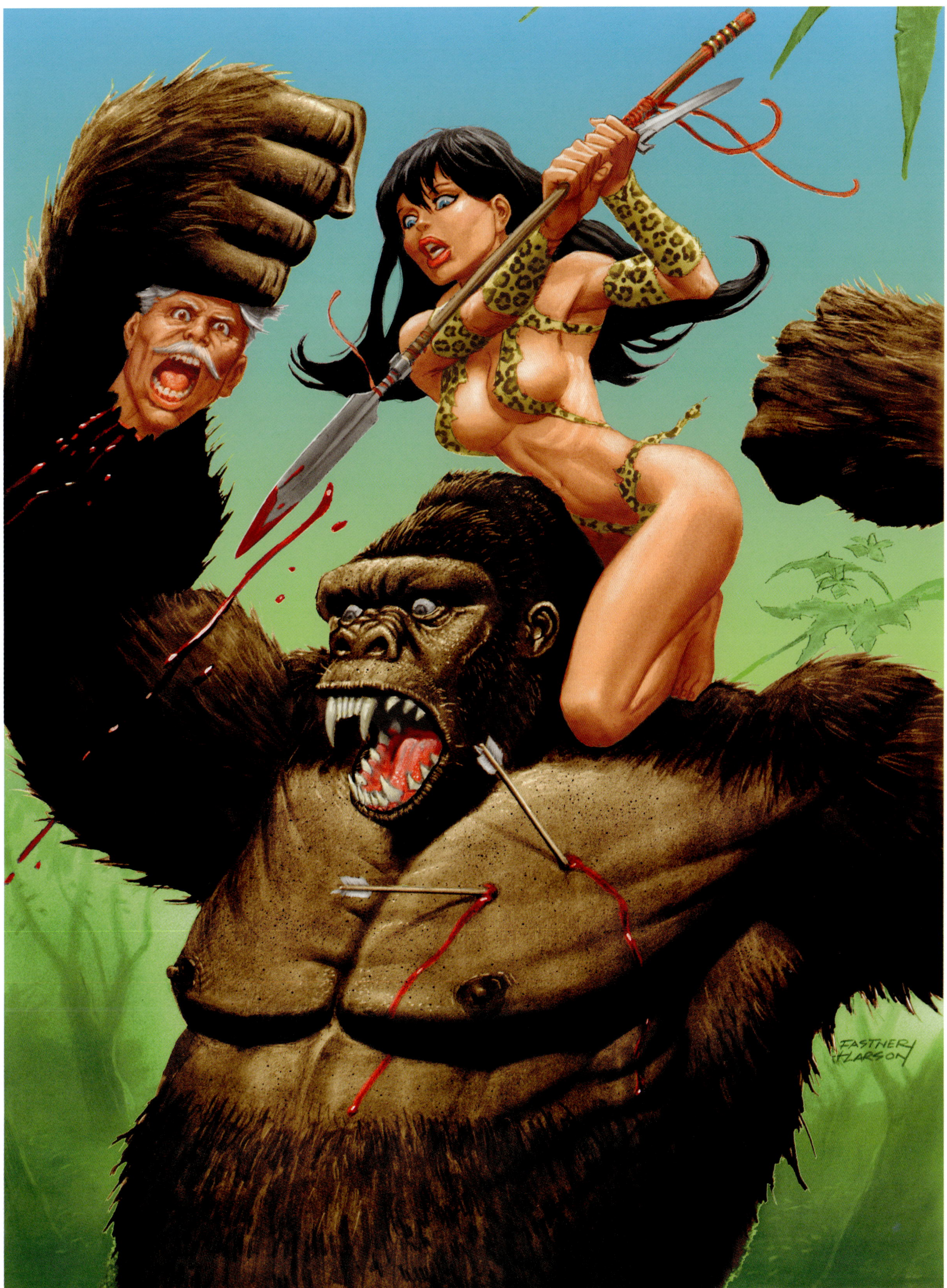

Teamwork

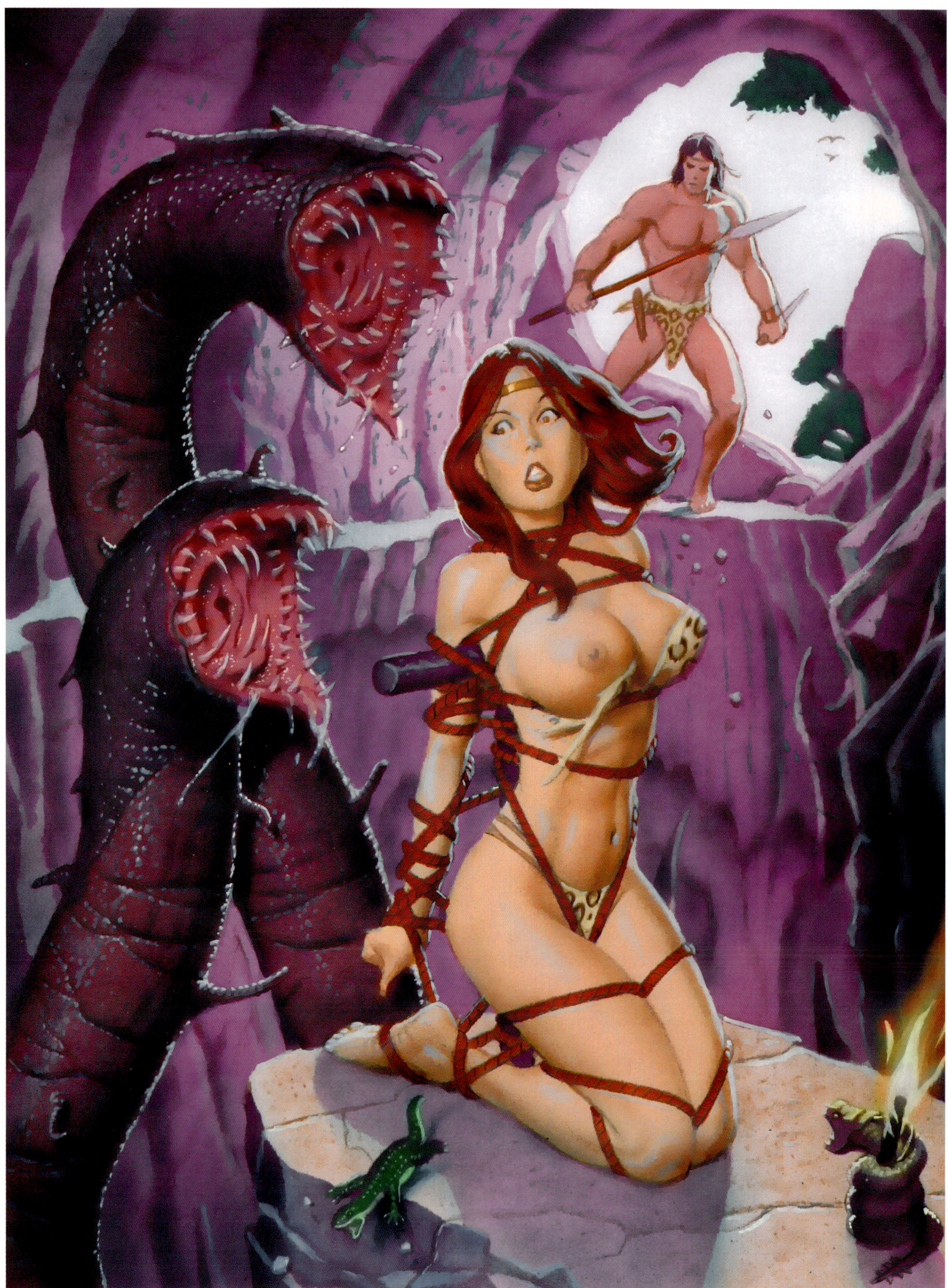

Cave Dwellers

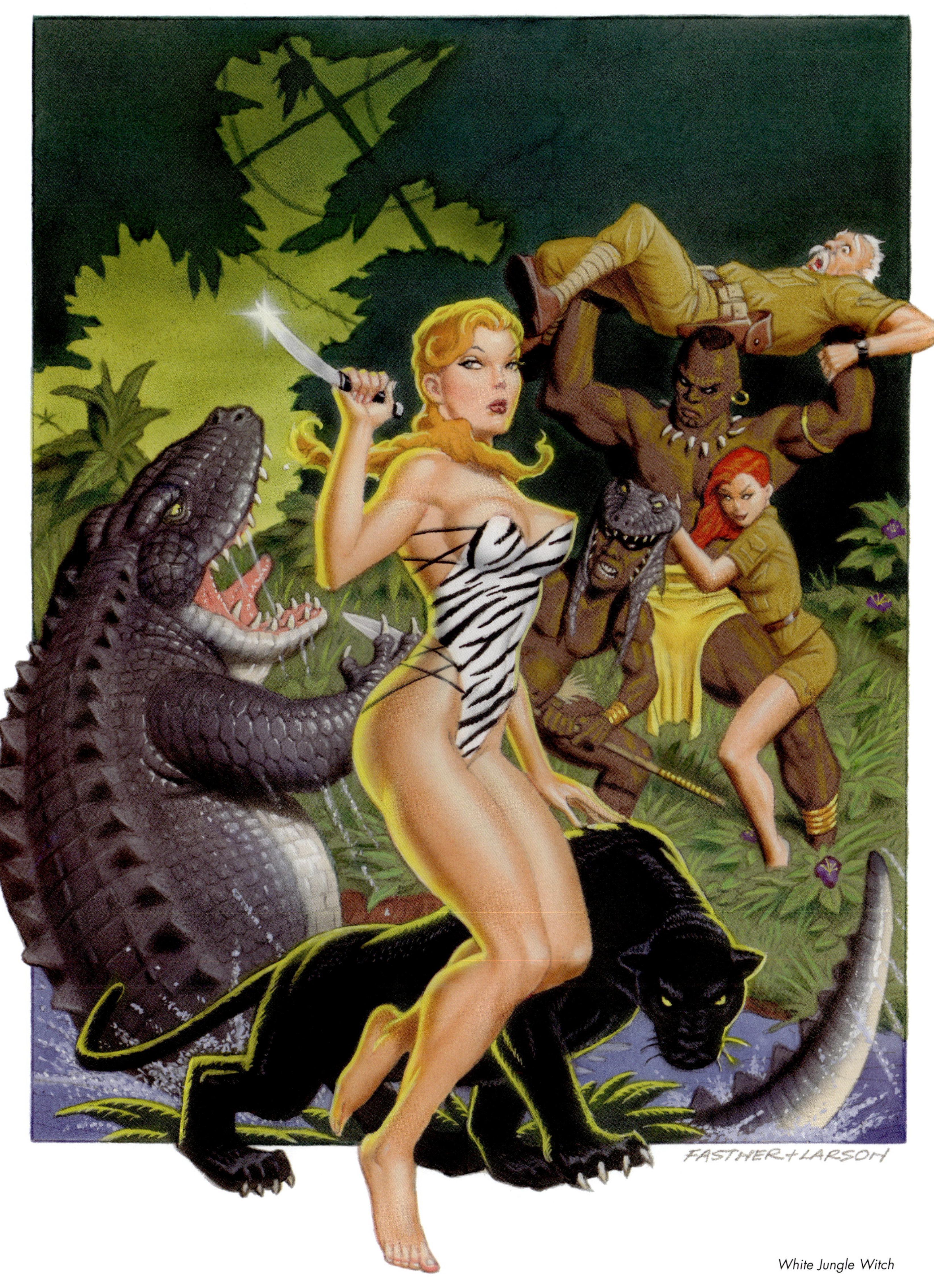

White Jungle Witch

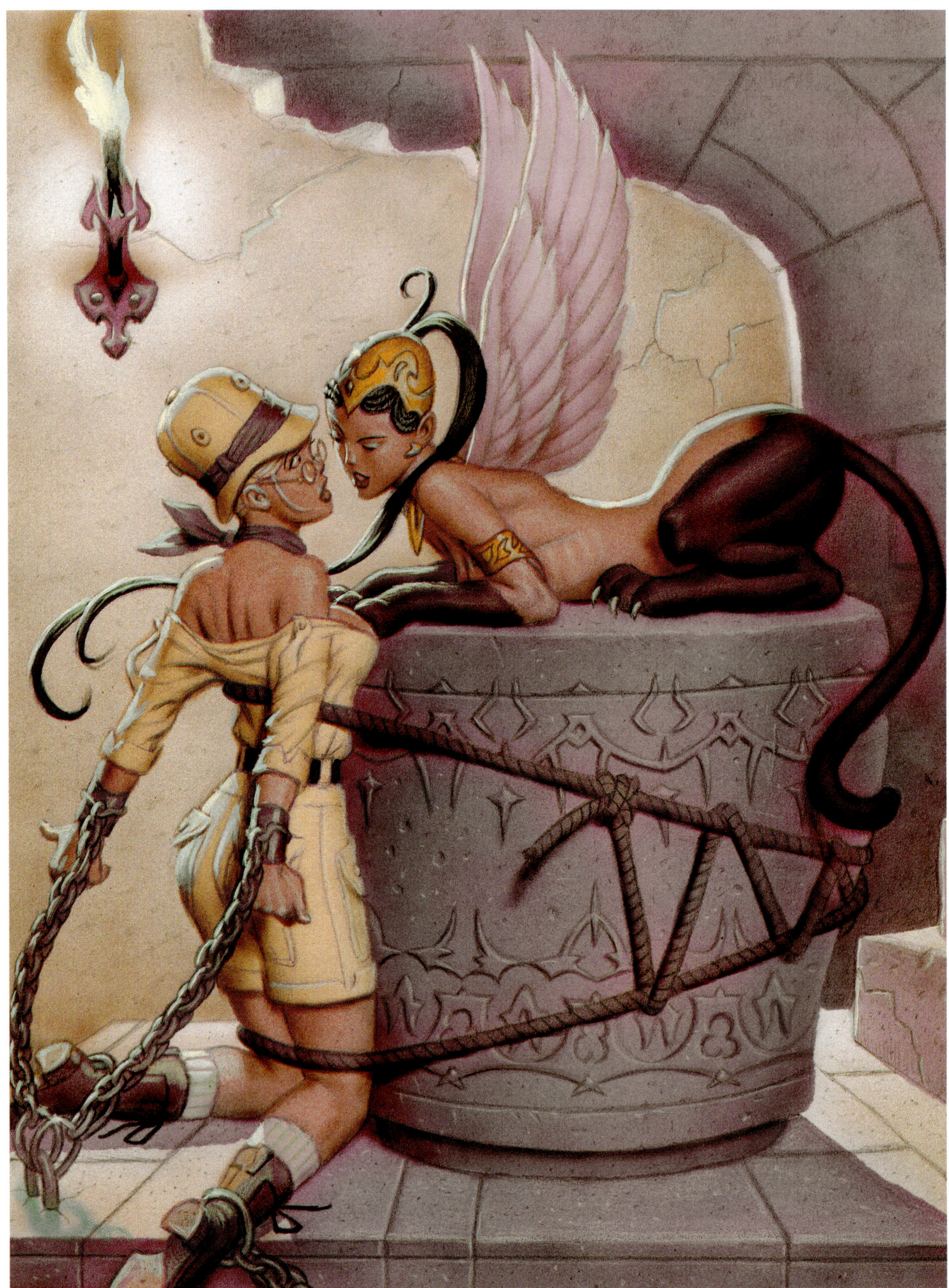

Bast in Heat

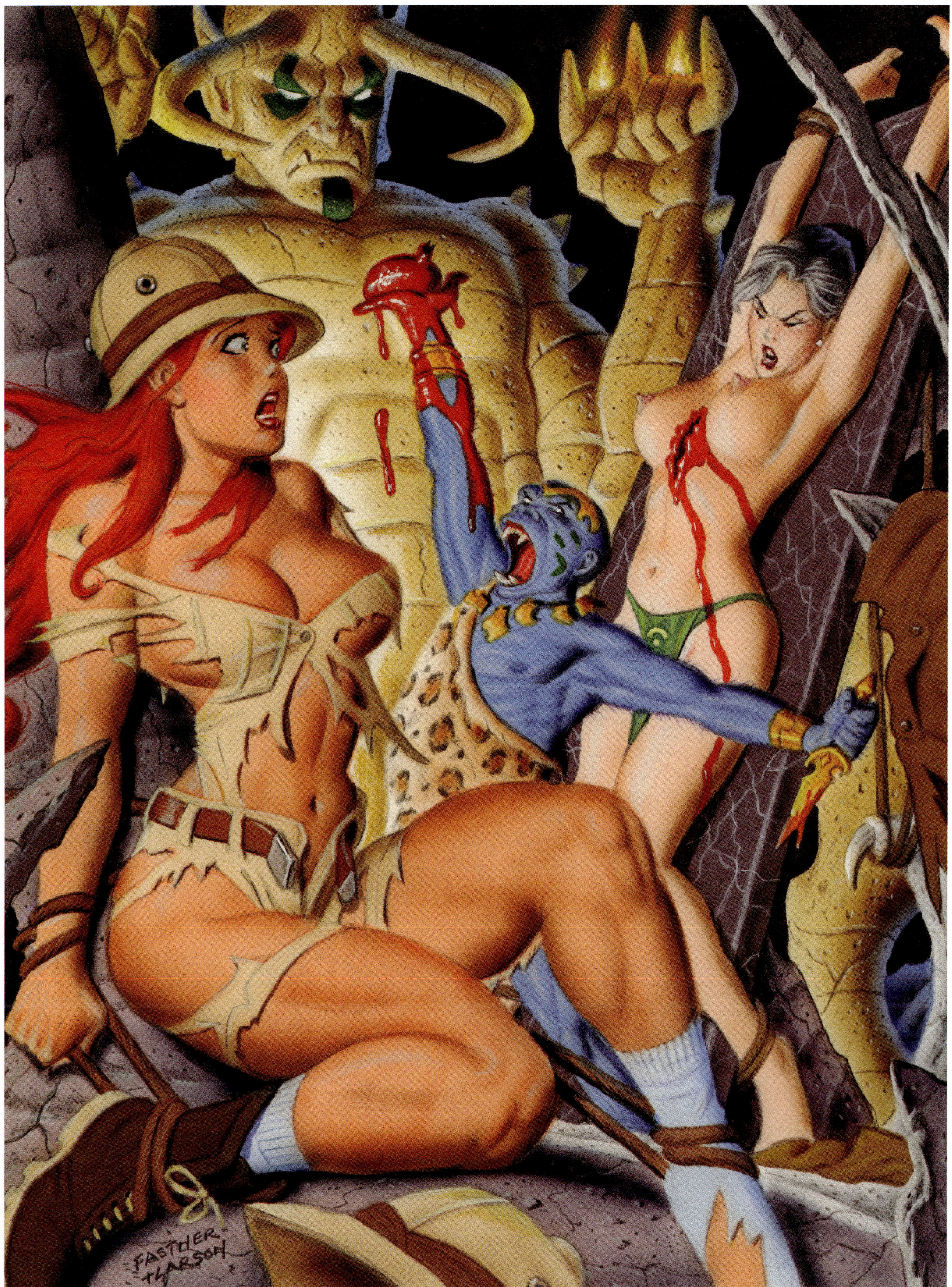

Temple of Blue Men

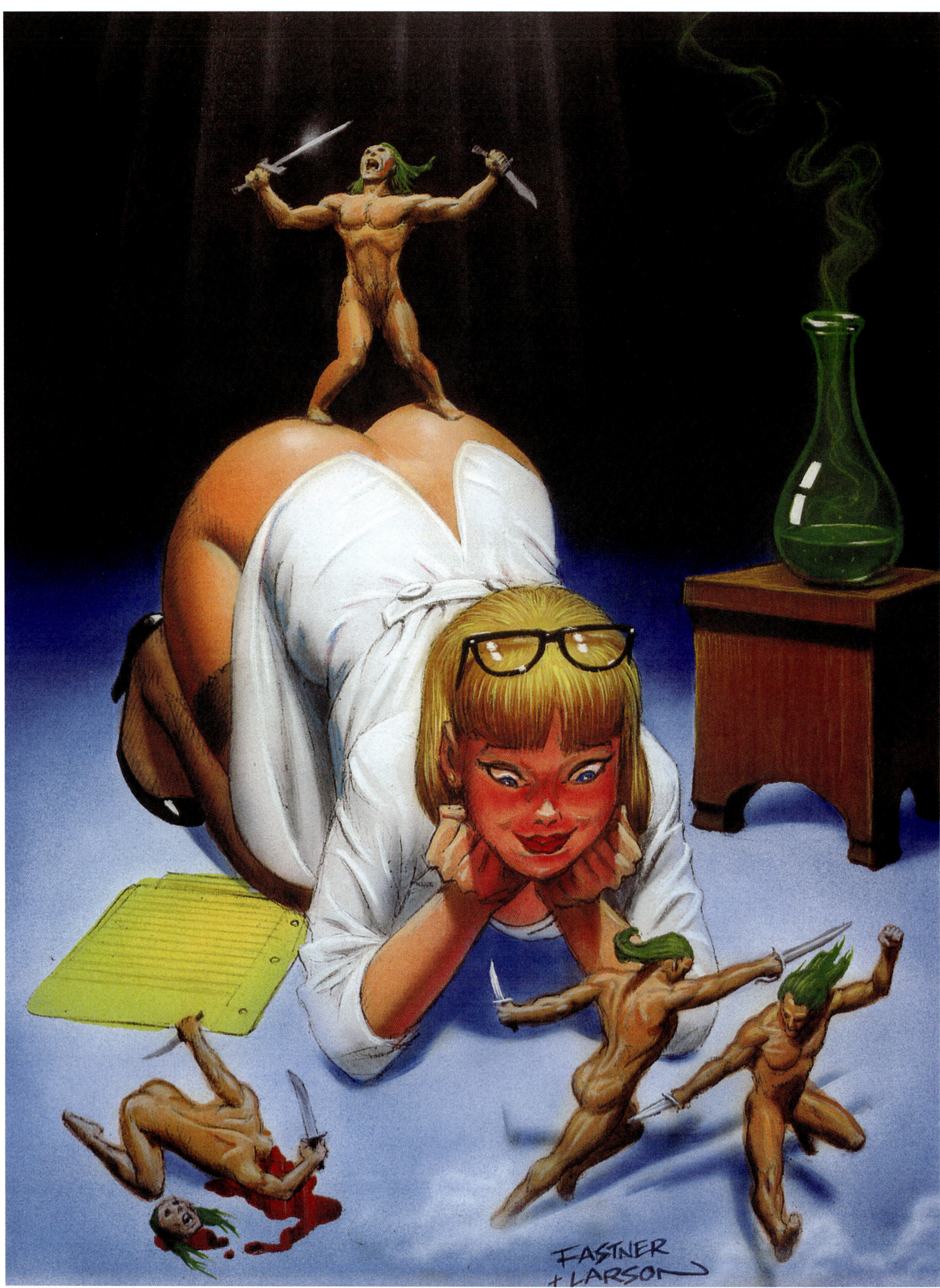

Boy's Night Out

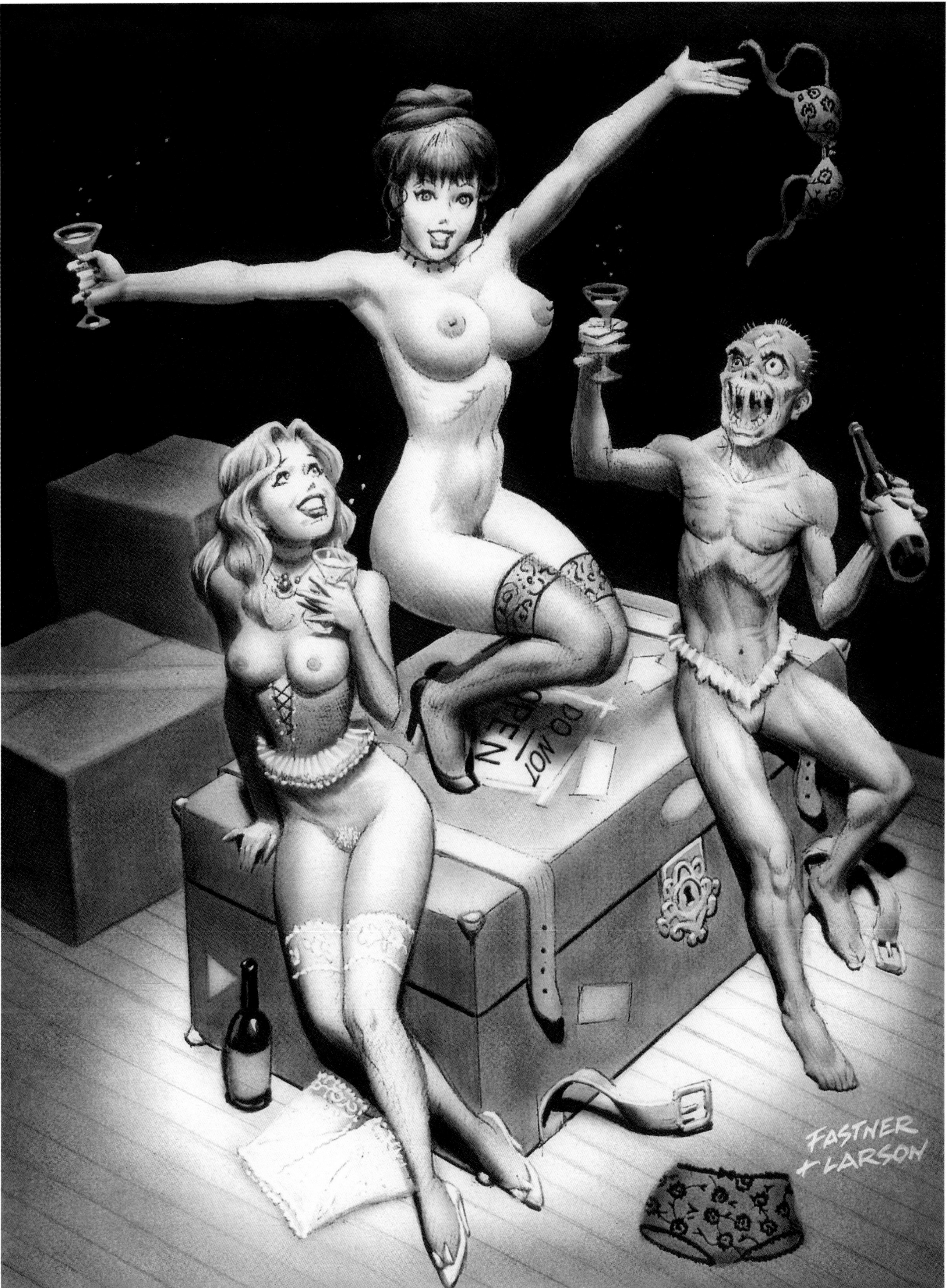

Toys in the Attic

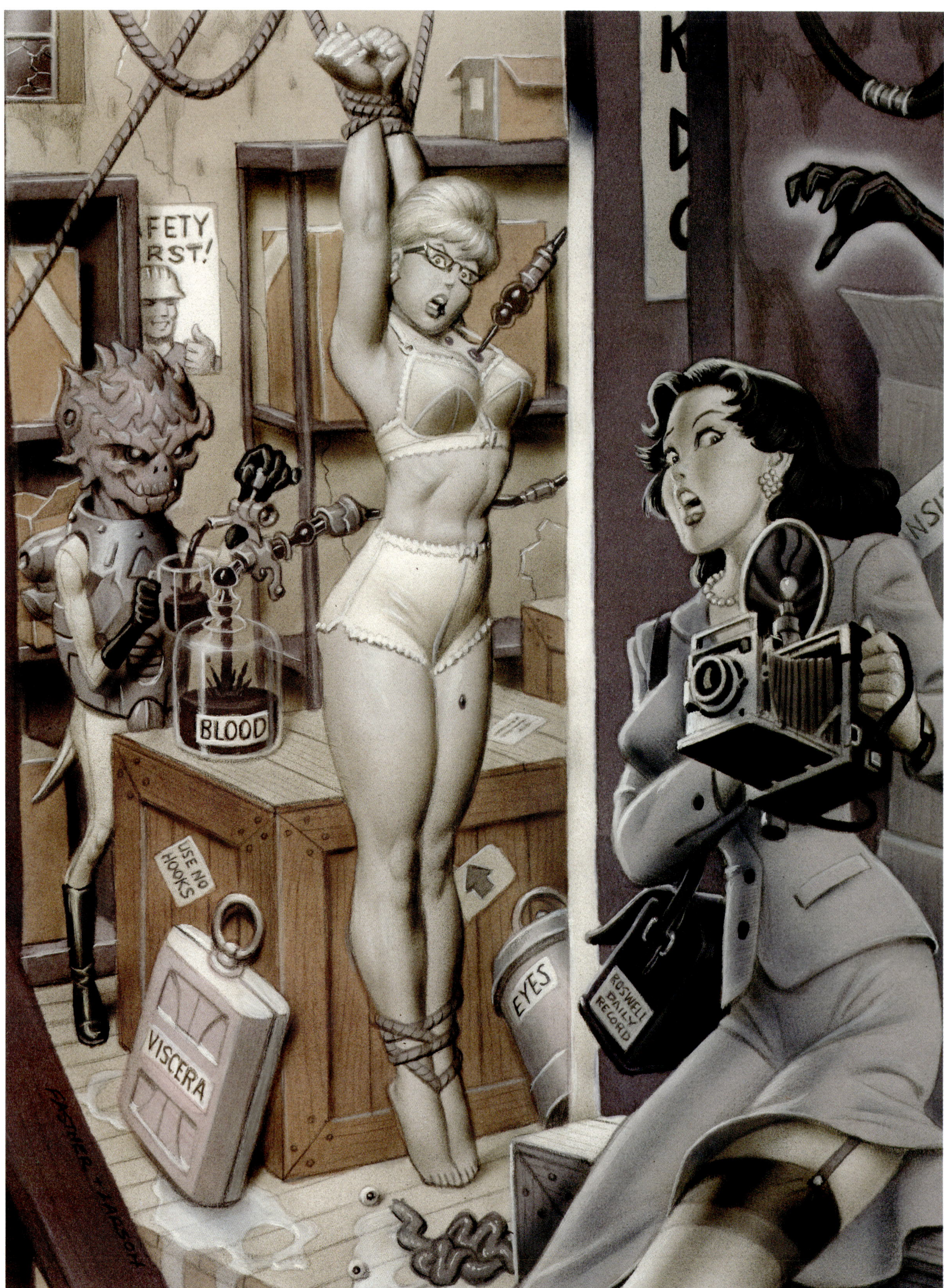

Breaking News at Roswell U-Stor

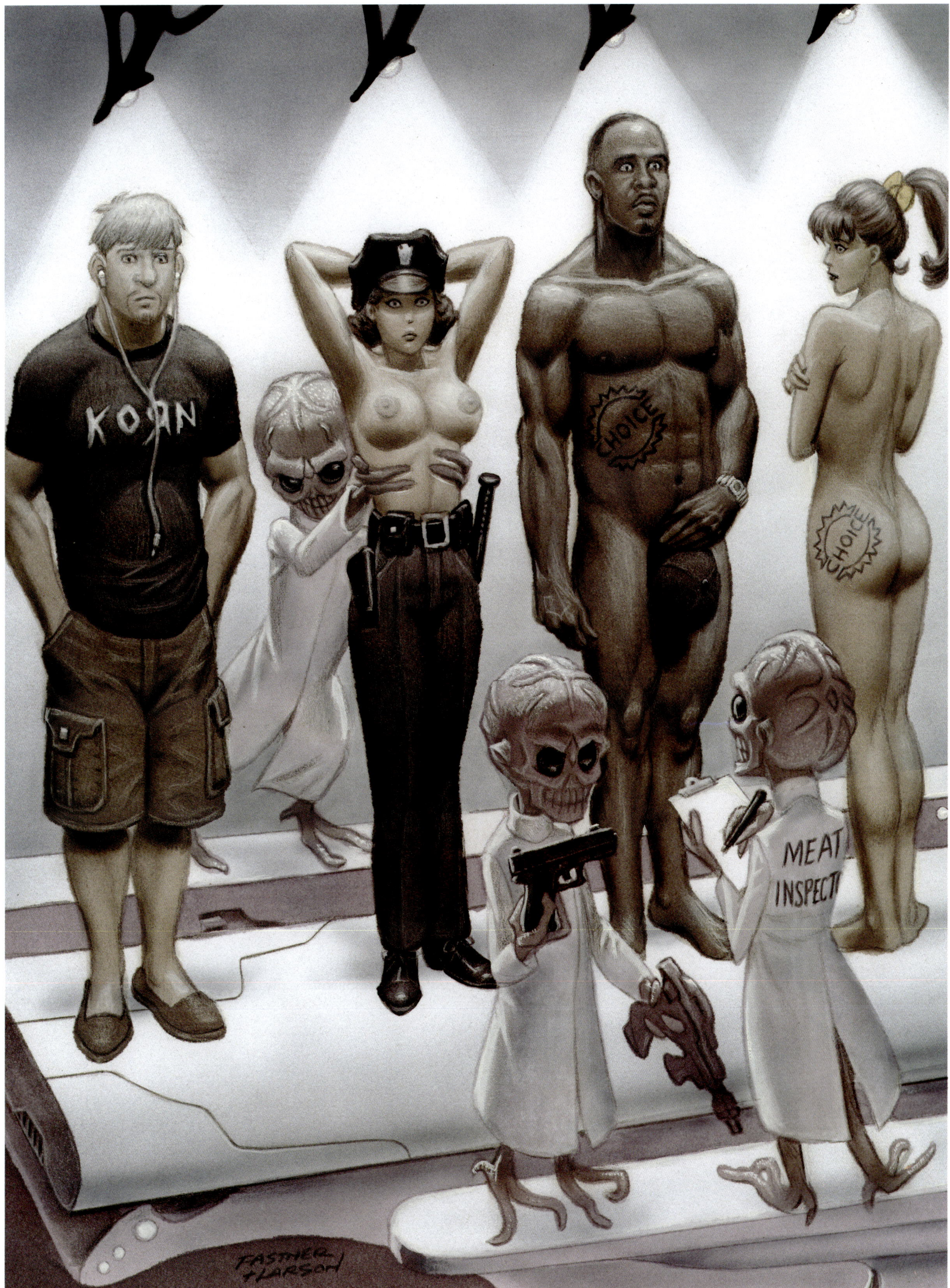

Cattle Call

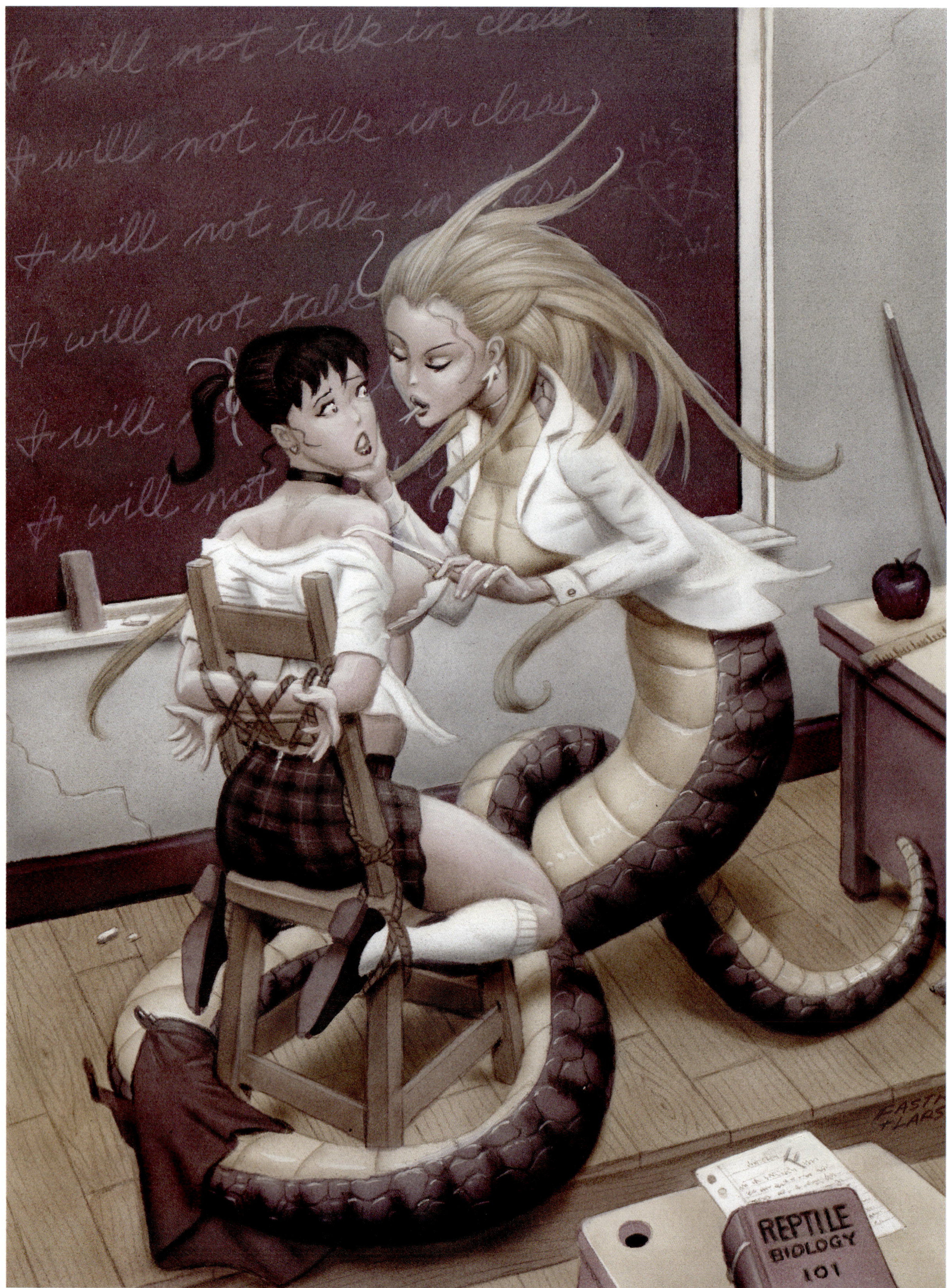

After Class

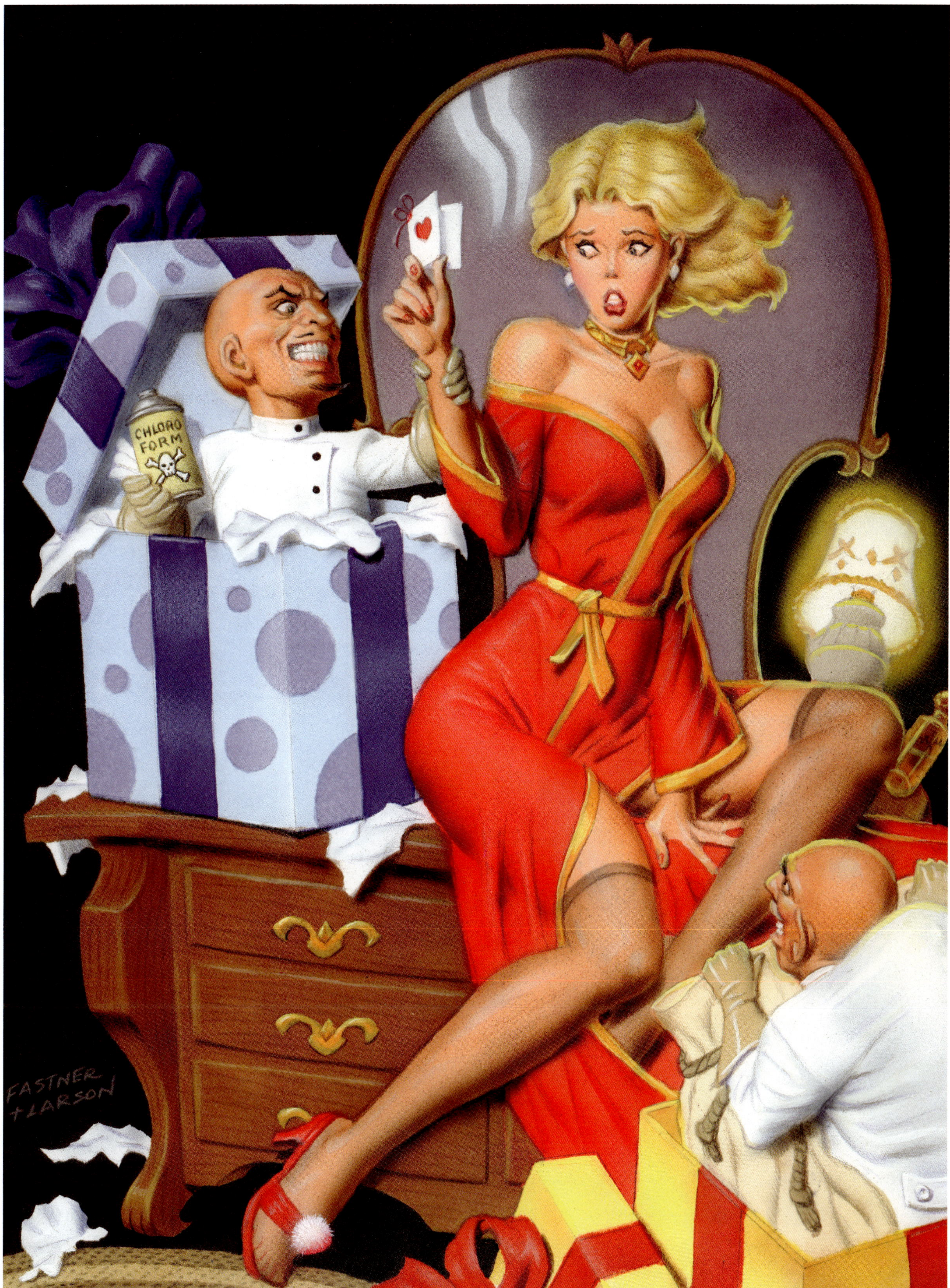

Surprise Package

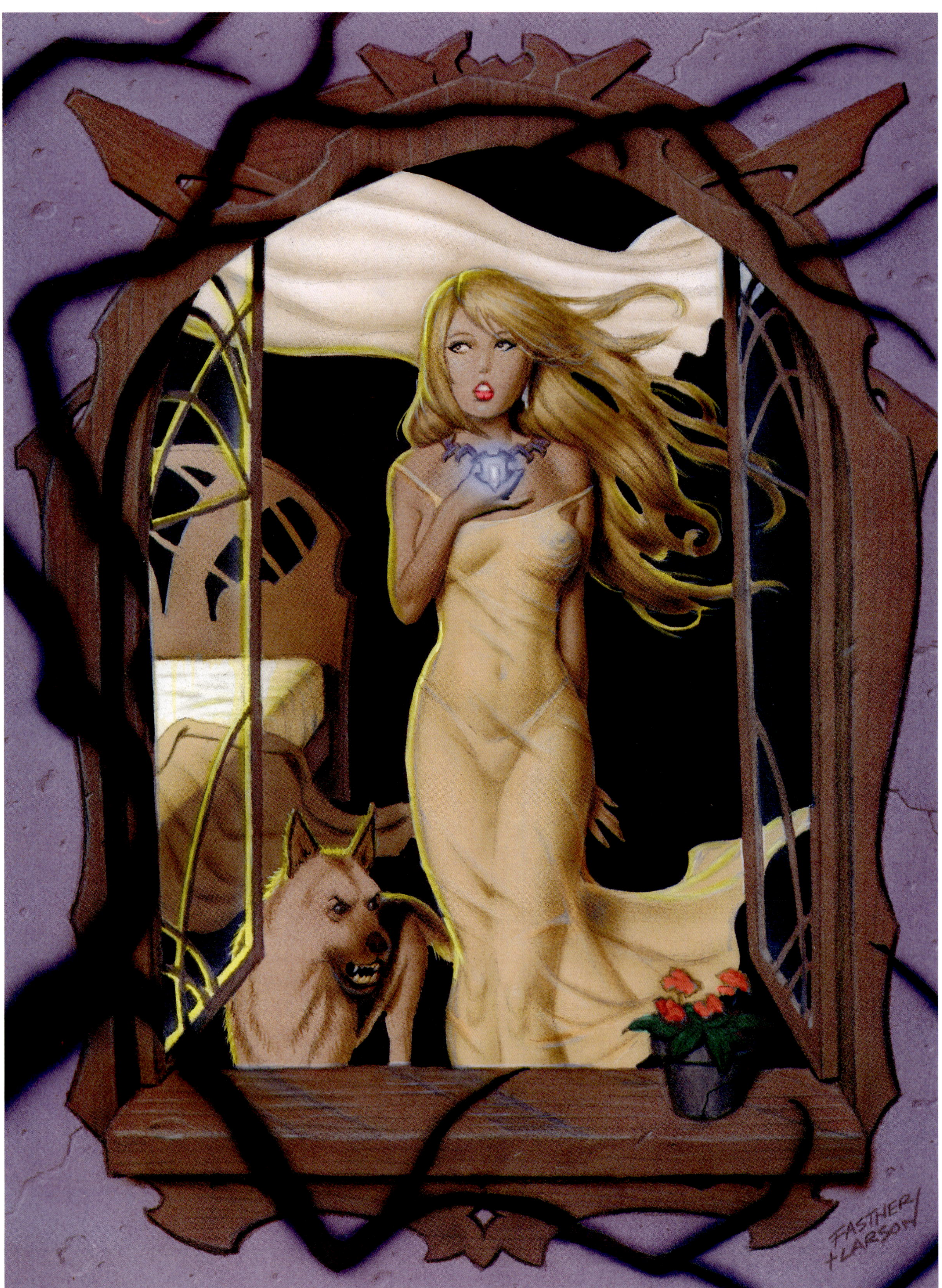

The Gathering Storm

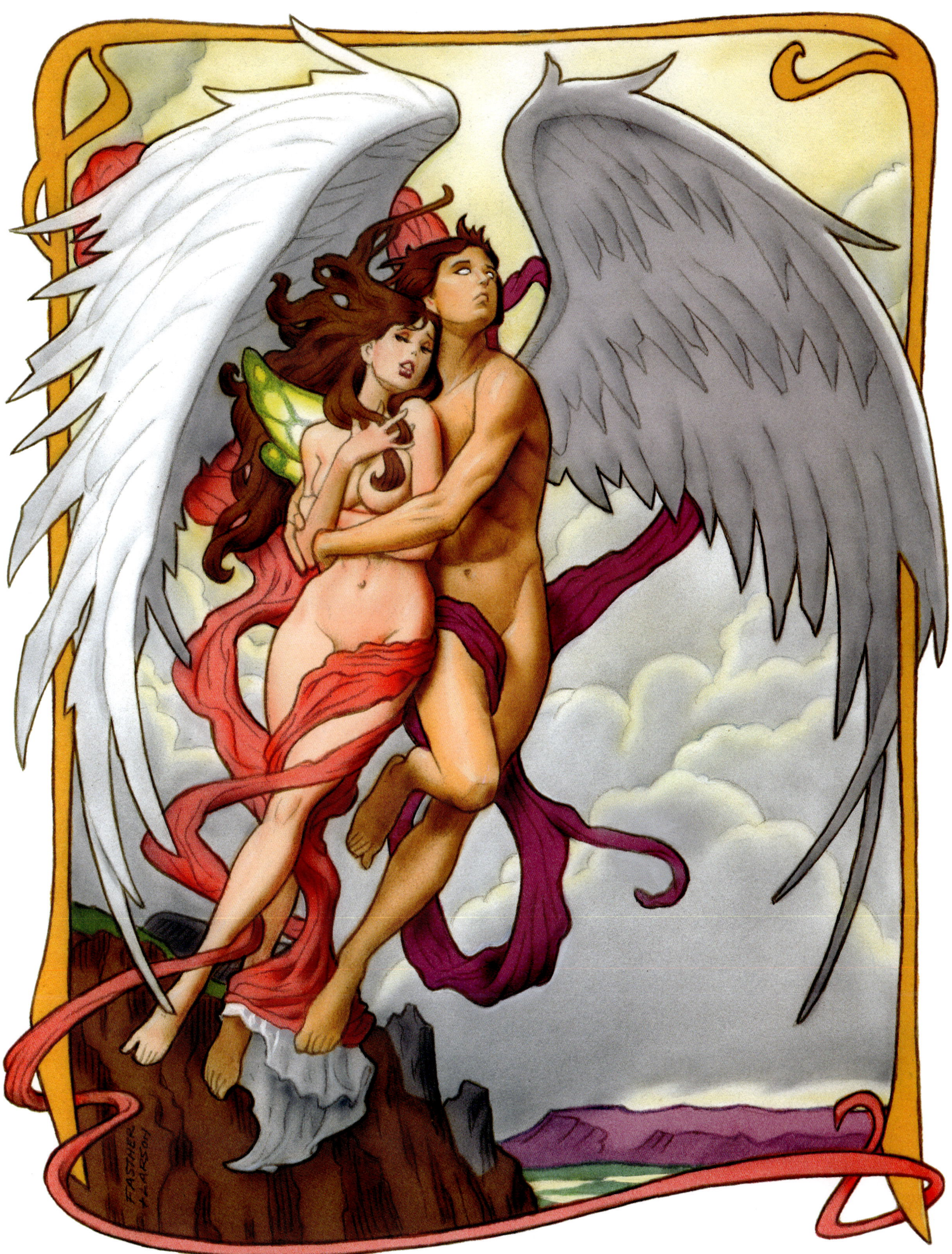

Heavenward

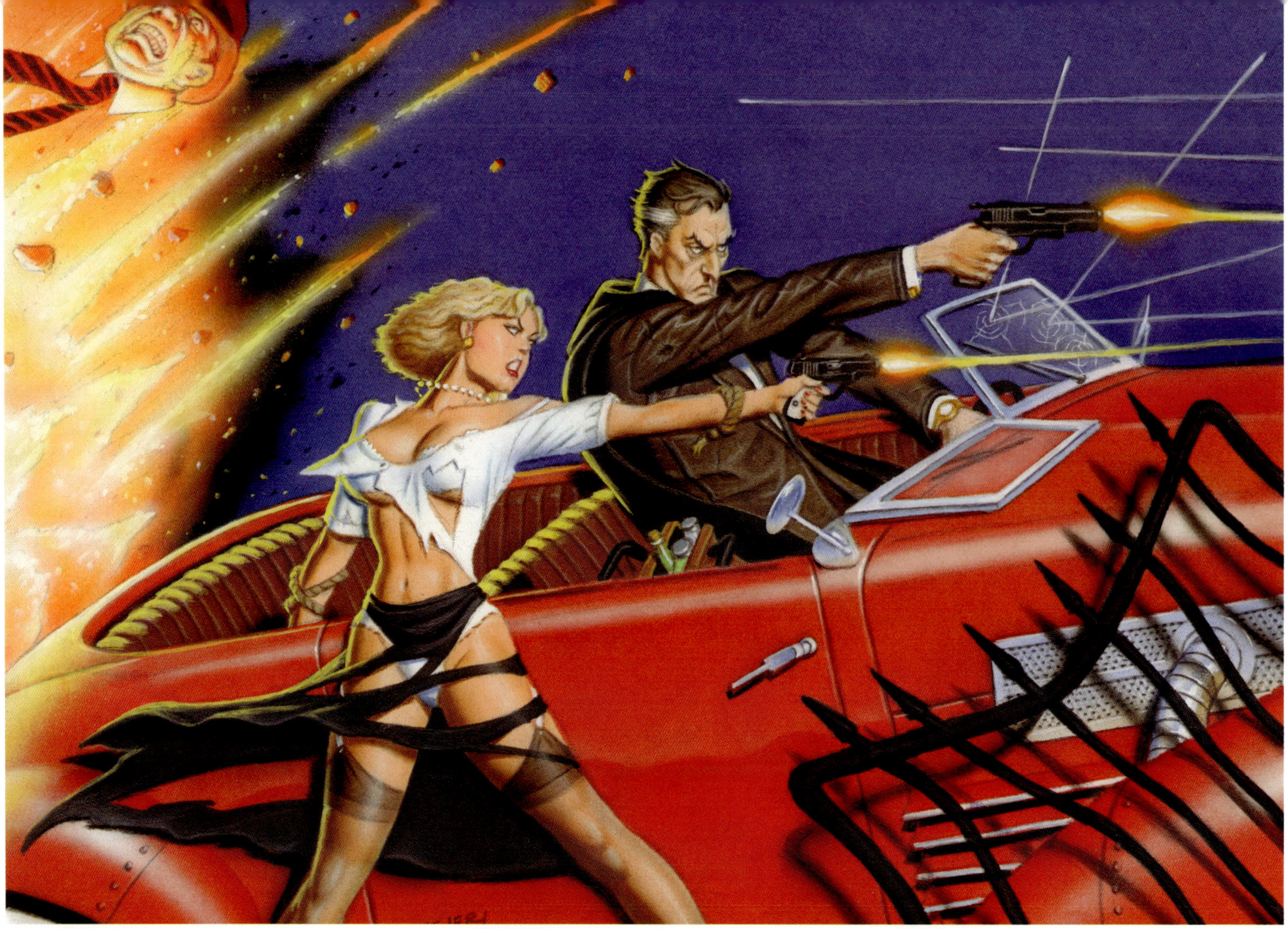

The Getaway

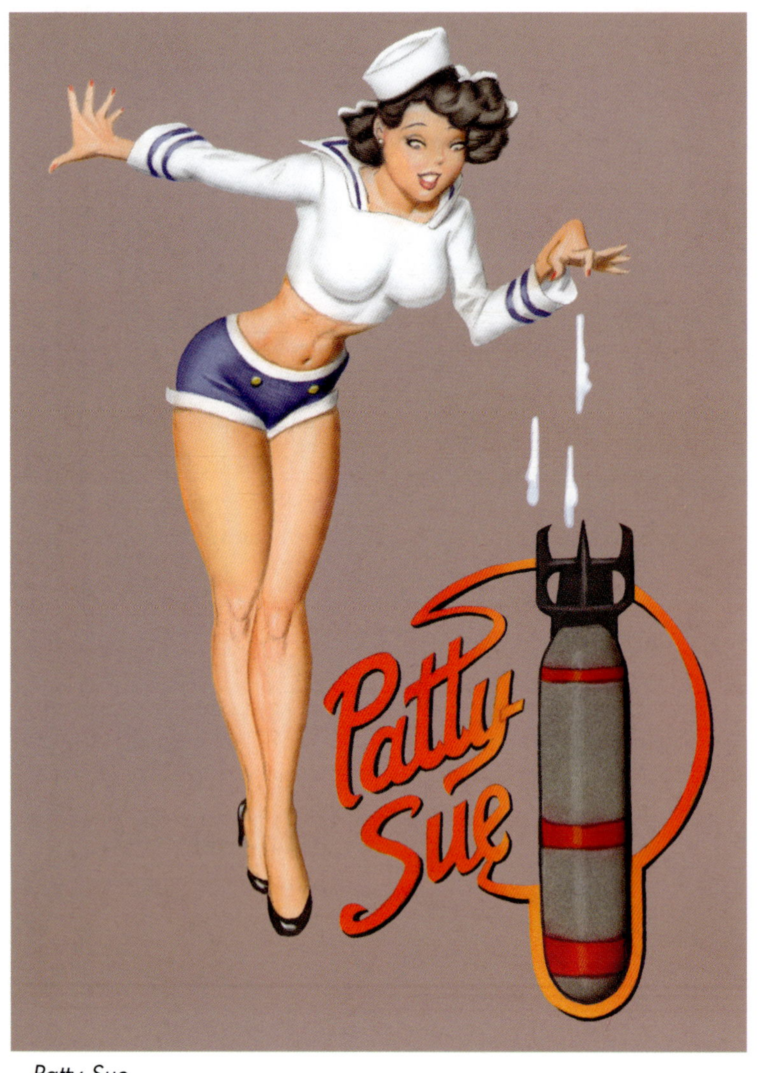

Patty Sue

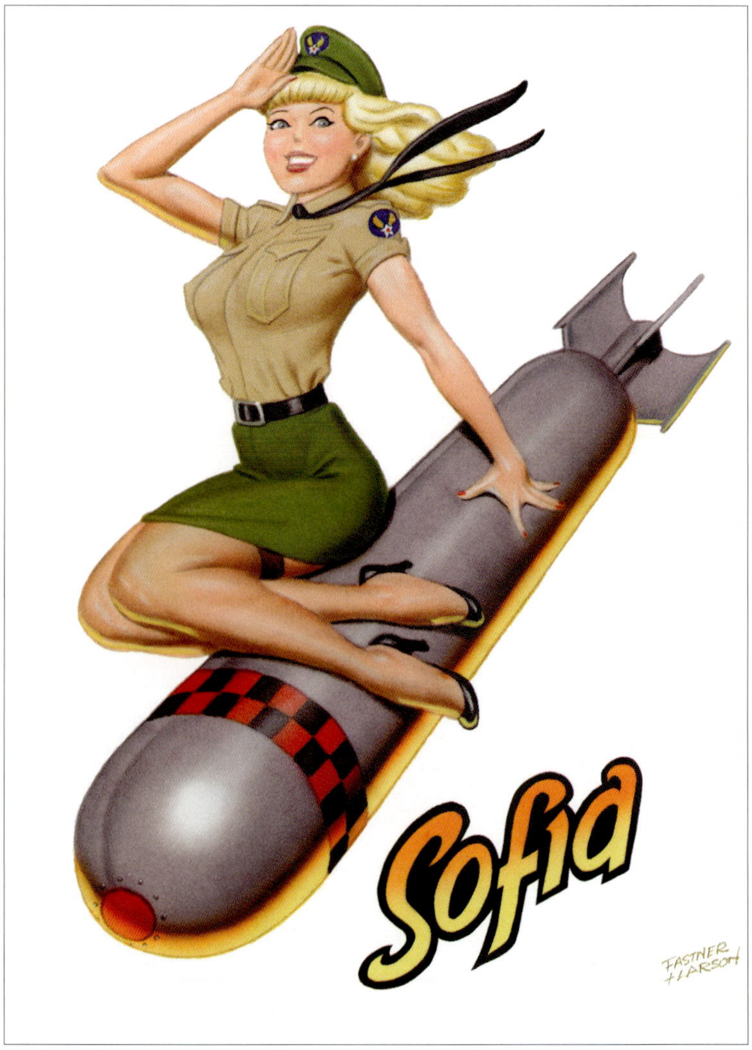

Sofia

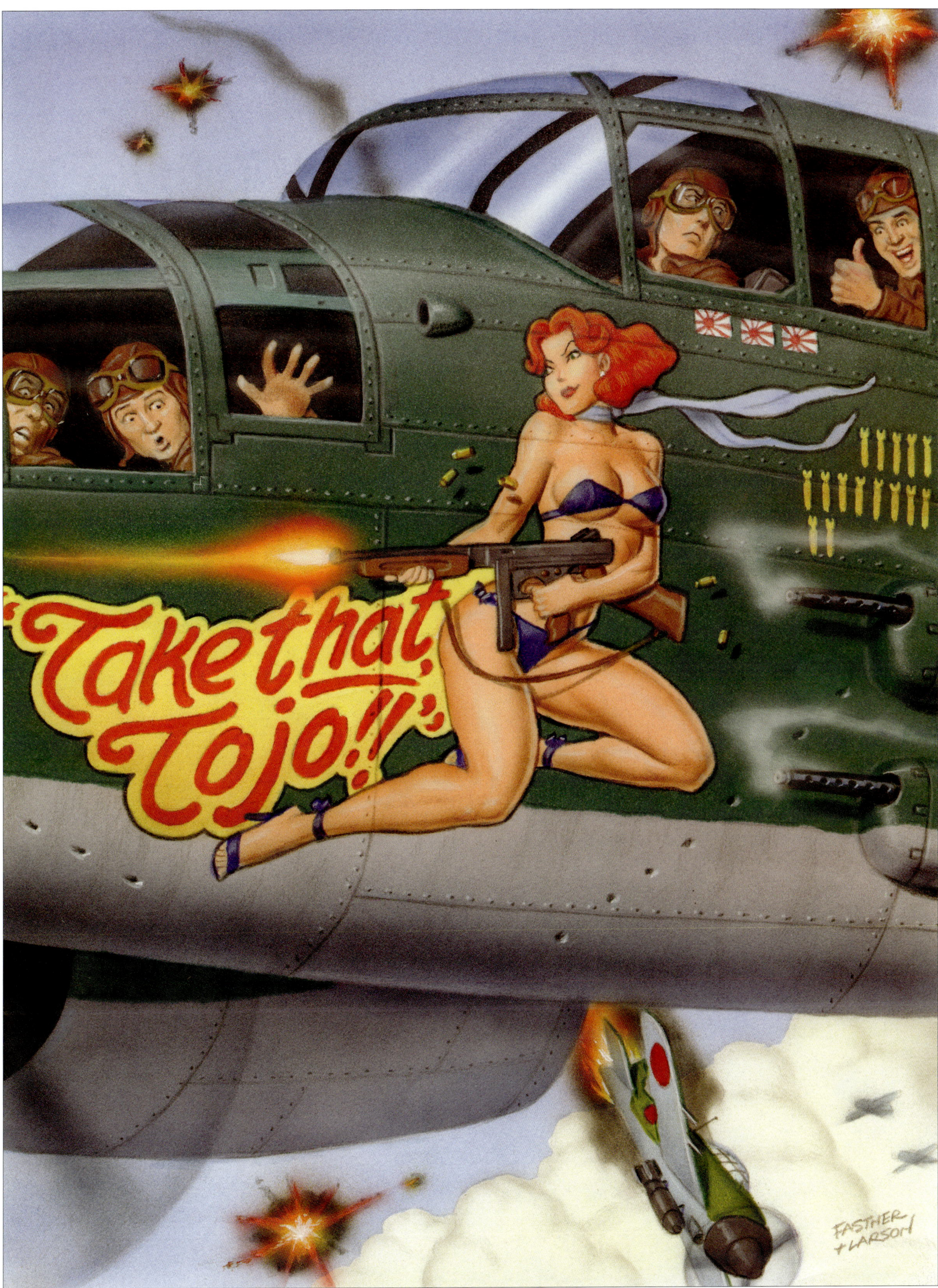

Take That, Tojo!

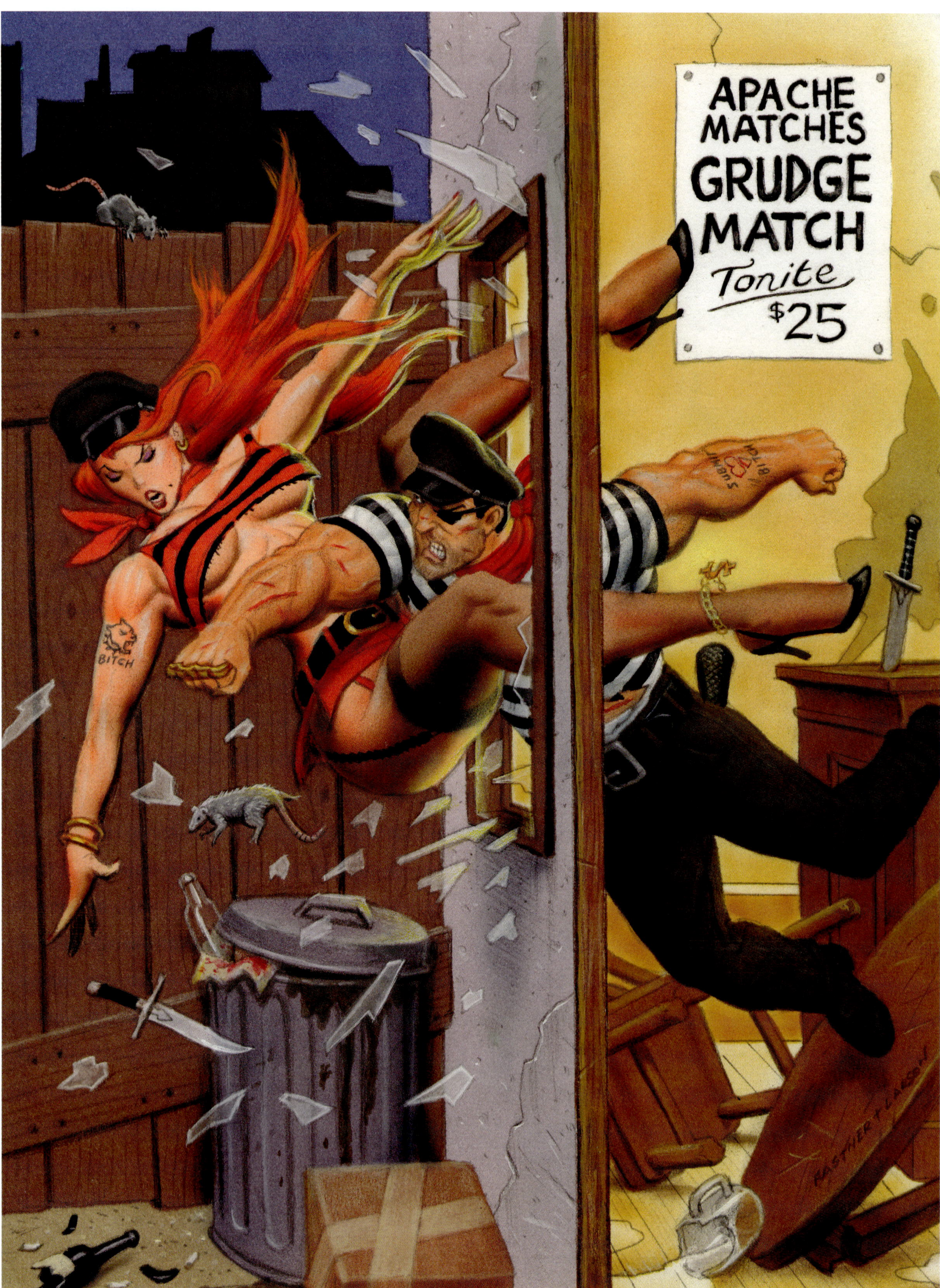

Window Pain

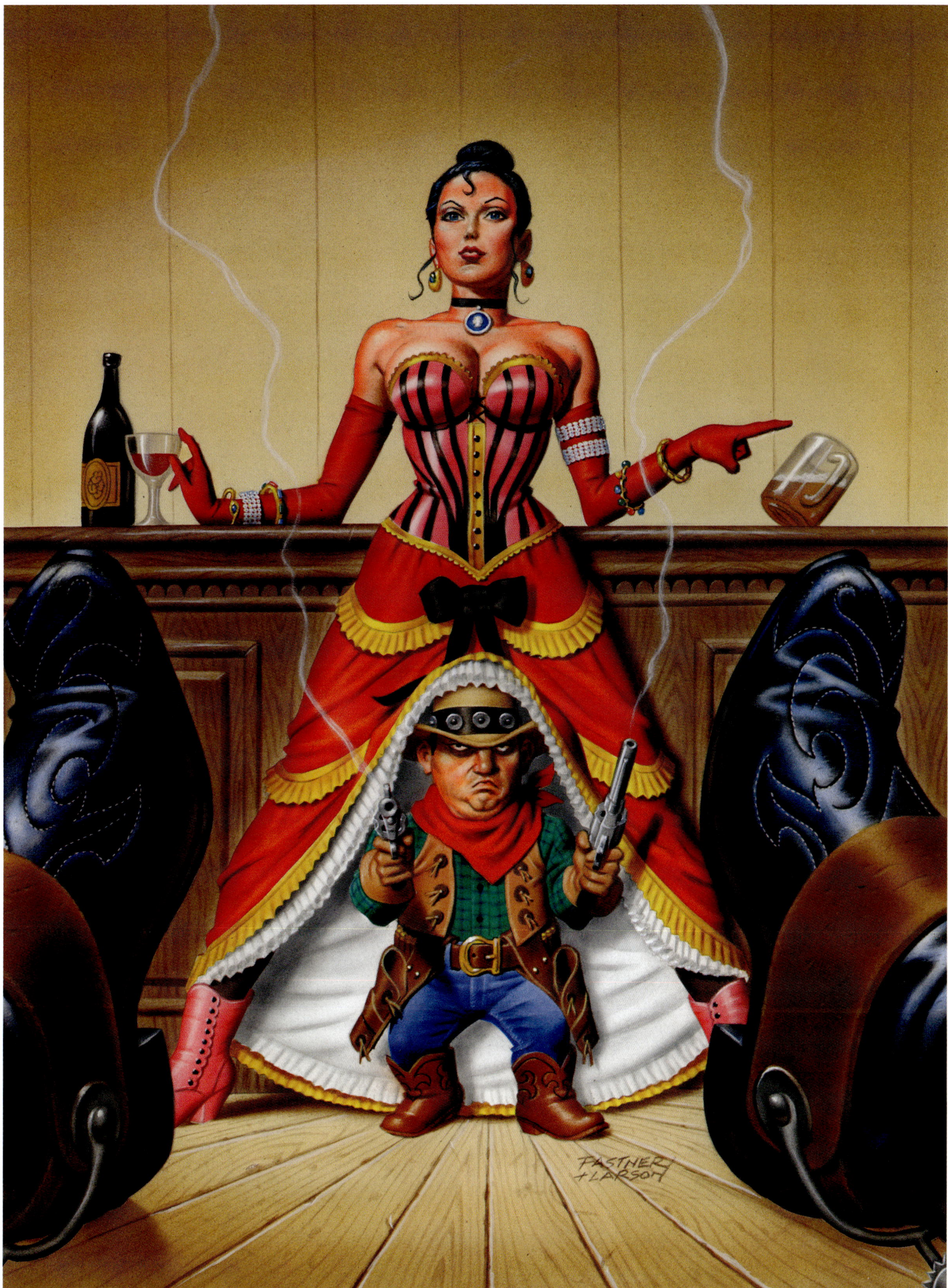

Low Noon

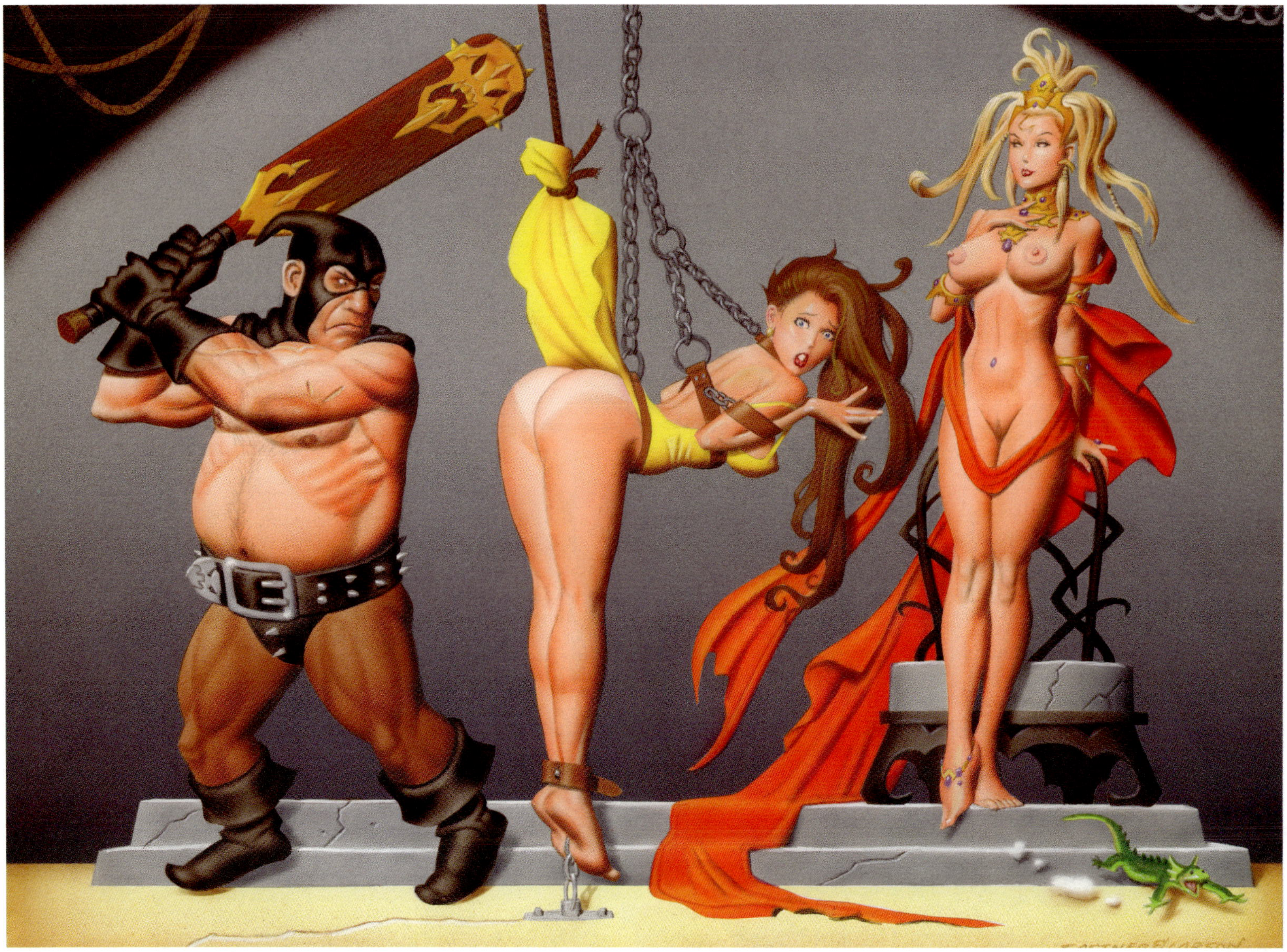

The Time Traveler's Predicament

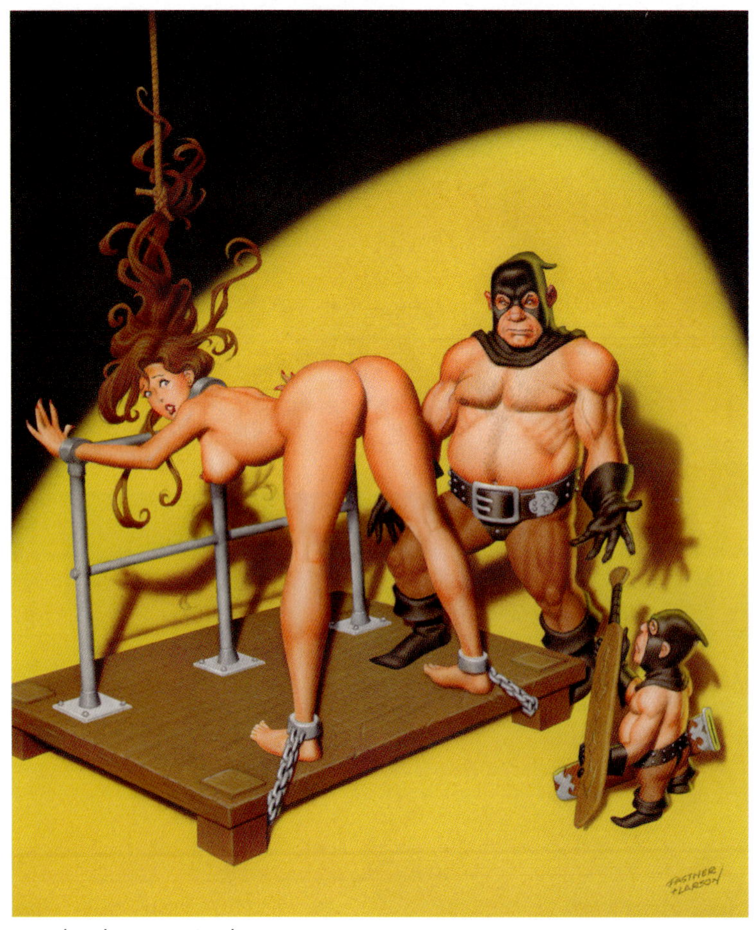

Behind in His Work

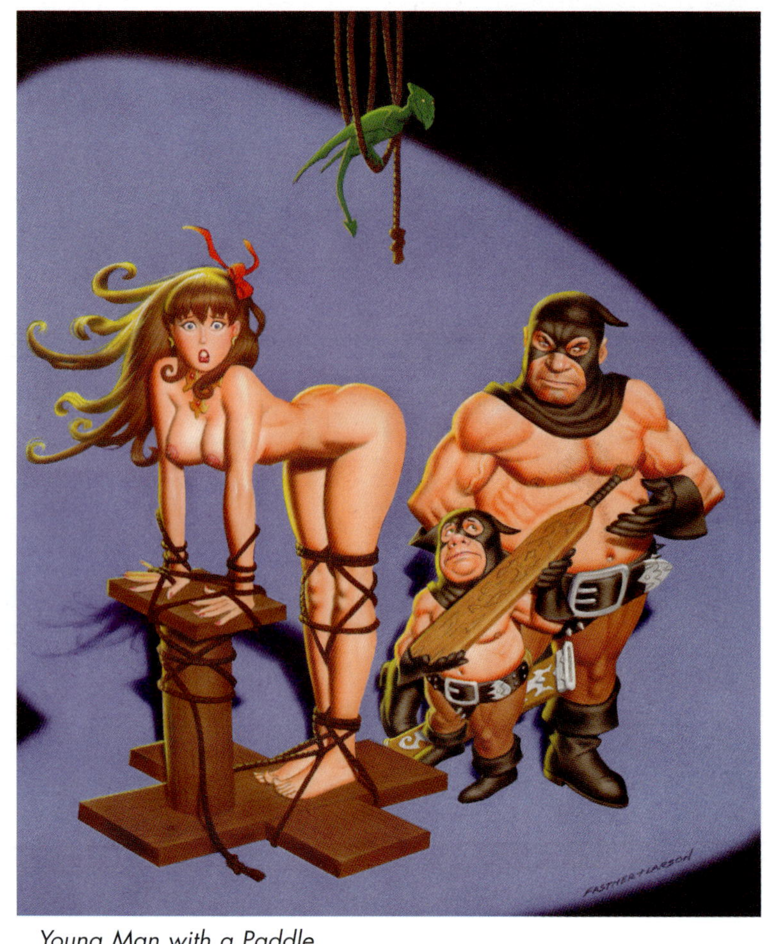

Young Man with a Paddle

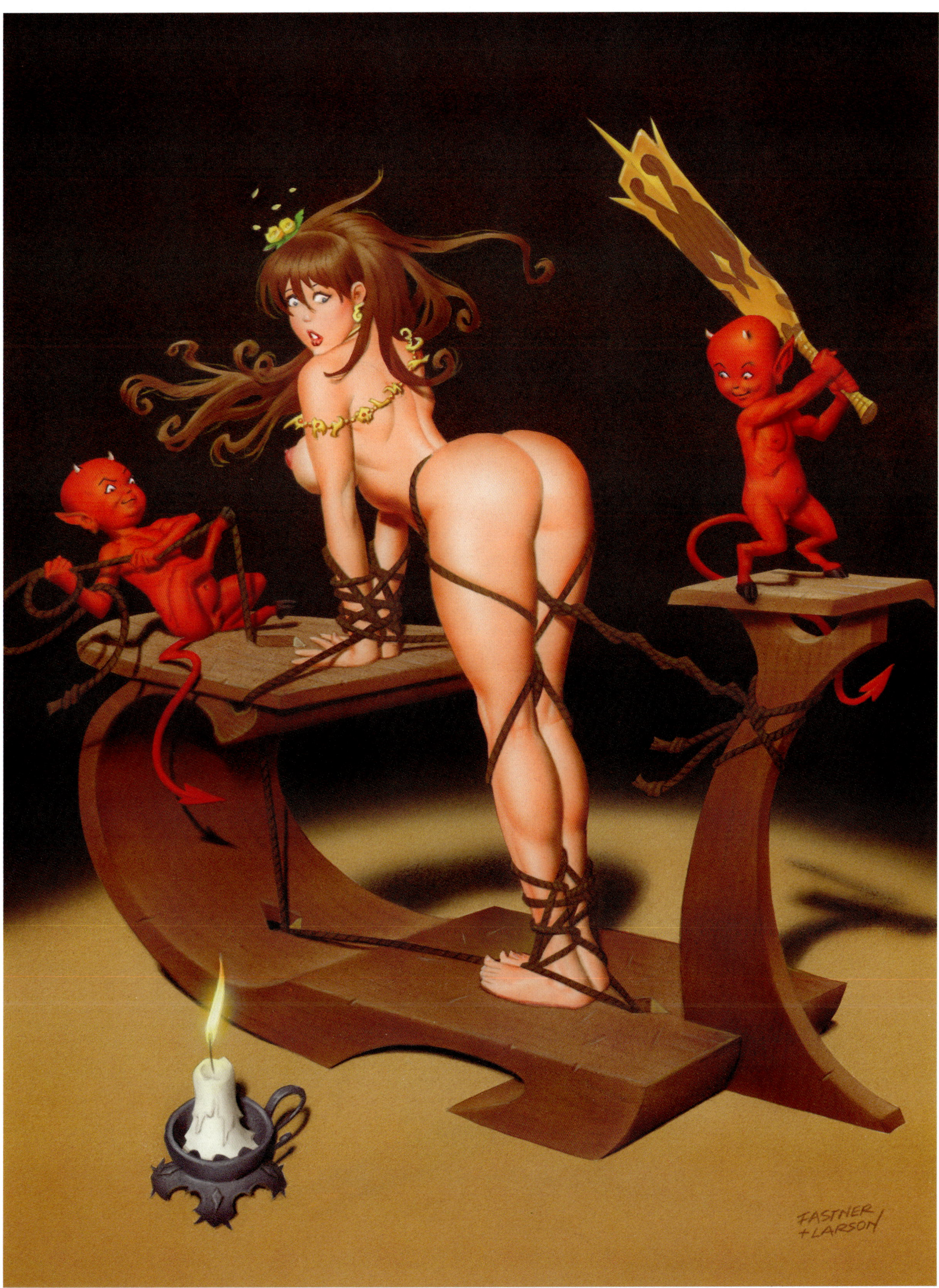

Spanking Machine

One Beauty, Two Beasts, and Several Steps to a Finished Painting

Fastner & Larson detail the details in creating the original painting "Hangin' Around"

Steve developed this marker and airbrush painting technique to save time by eliminating the pencil drawing transfer step and most of the tedious frisketing involved in traditional airbrushing.

Steve makes a clean, light 8.5" x 11" scan of Rich's pencil drawing, and colors it with markers. He then applies airbrush color. Finally, he adds fine details with color pencil, and also watercolor, gouache and ink applied with a #3 sable brush.

Since the painting is done on thin paper, the tricky part is to avoid brushing on too much wet paint, causing the paper to ripple and curl. Paints have to be applied lightly and slowly, allowing adequate time to dry between coats.

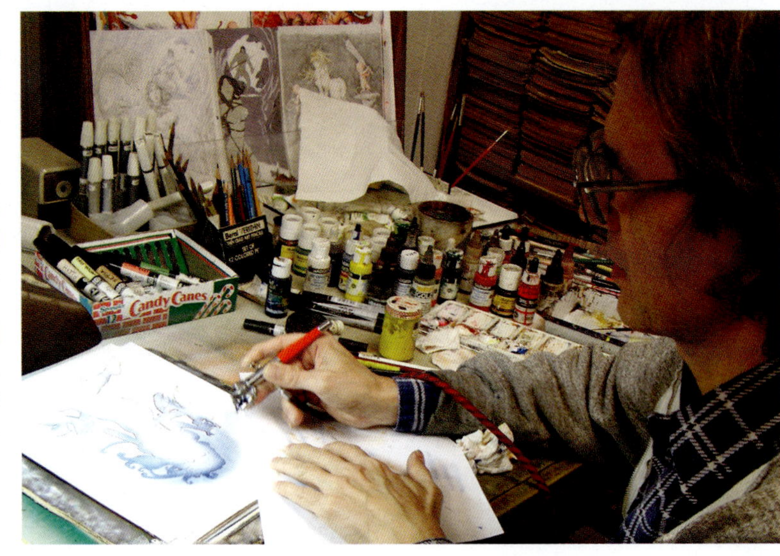

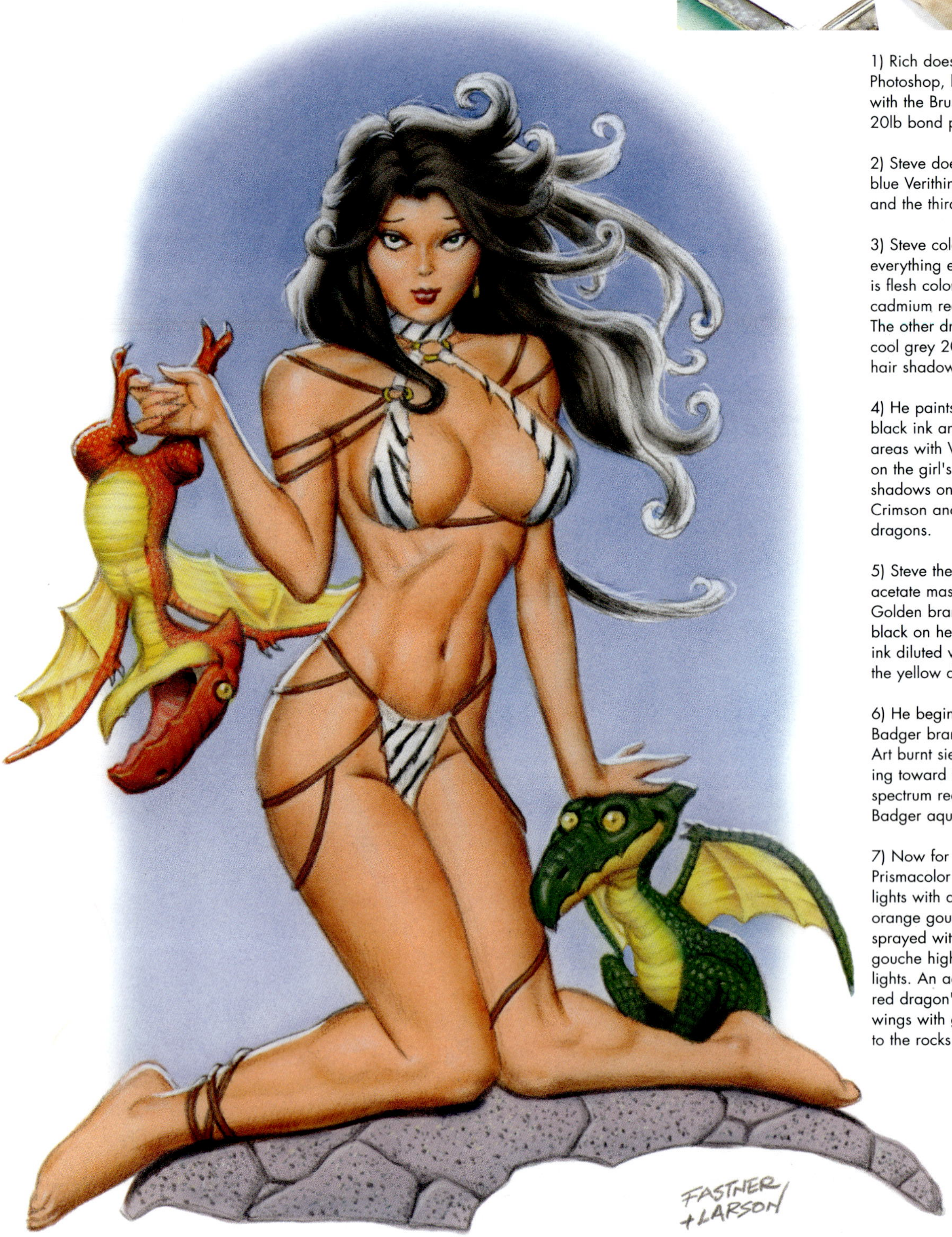

1) Rich does a tight pencil drawing. Steve scans it into Photoshop, lightens it with Brightness/Contrast, and cleans it up with the Brush and Eraser tools. He then prints out 3 copies on 20lb bond paper.

2) Steve does a color pencil study on one copy, using black and blue Verithin pencils. (The second copy is used in a paper mask, and the third is used for the finished art.)

3) Steve colors the art copy with markers. He uses AD brand for everything except the rocks, which is Prismacolor. The girl's skin is flesh color, and her leather straps are sepia. The left dragon is cadmium red (with a salmon colored mouth) and pale yellow. The other dragon is nile green and pale yellow. The rocks are cool grey 20%. Black color pencil is used to indicate the girl's hair shadows and the zebra stripes on her bikini.

4) He paints the girl's eyes and lips with a sable brush, using black ink and Dr. Martin's watercolors. He blocks in the shadow areas with Verithin color pencils, using dark umber for shadows on the girl's skin and the dragons' yellow areas, and black for shadows on the red and green dragon, and on the rocks. Crimson and green pencils are used for the scales on the dragons.

5) Steve then airbrushes the shadows, using a small homemade acetate mask for sharp edges and to prevent overspray. He uses Golden brand raw umber for the girl's skin shadows, and blue black on her bikini. Shadows on the dragons are sprayed black ink diluted with water. The girl's hair is sprayed black ink, and the yellow dragon shaded areas are sprayed raw umber.

6) He begins to airbrush the non-shadow areas, spraying a little Badger brand crimson to color the girl's cheeks, and some Com-Art burnt sienna, starting at the outer edges of her skin and blending toward the center. The red dragon gets some Dr. Matin's spectrum red modeling, and the green dragon is airbrushed with Badger aqua.

7) Now for the highlights. Flesh highlights are spotted in with a Prismacolor white pencil. Steve then goes over the penciled highlights with a sable brush and a mixture of white and cadmium orange gouache. If they need smoothing out, the highlights are sprayed with gouache. The red dragon has yellow orange gouche highlights, and the green one has yellow green highlights. An additional white gouache highlight is sprayed on the red dragon's belly. Lines and wrinkles are added to the dragon's wings with gold watercolor and a sable brush. Spots are added to the rocks with black and white color pencil.

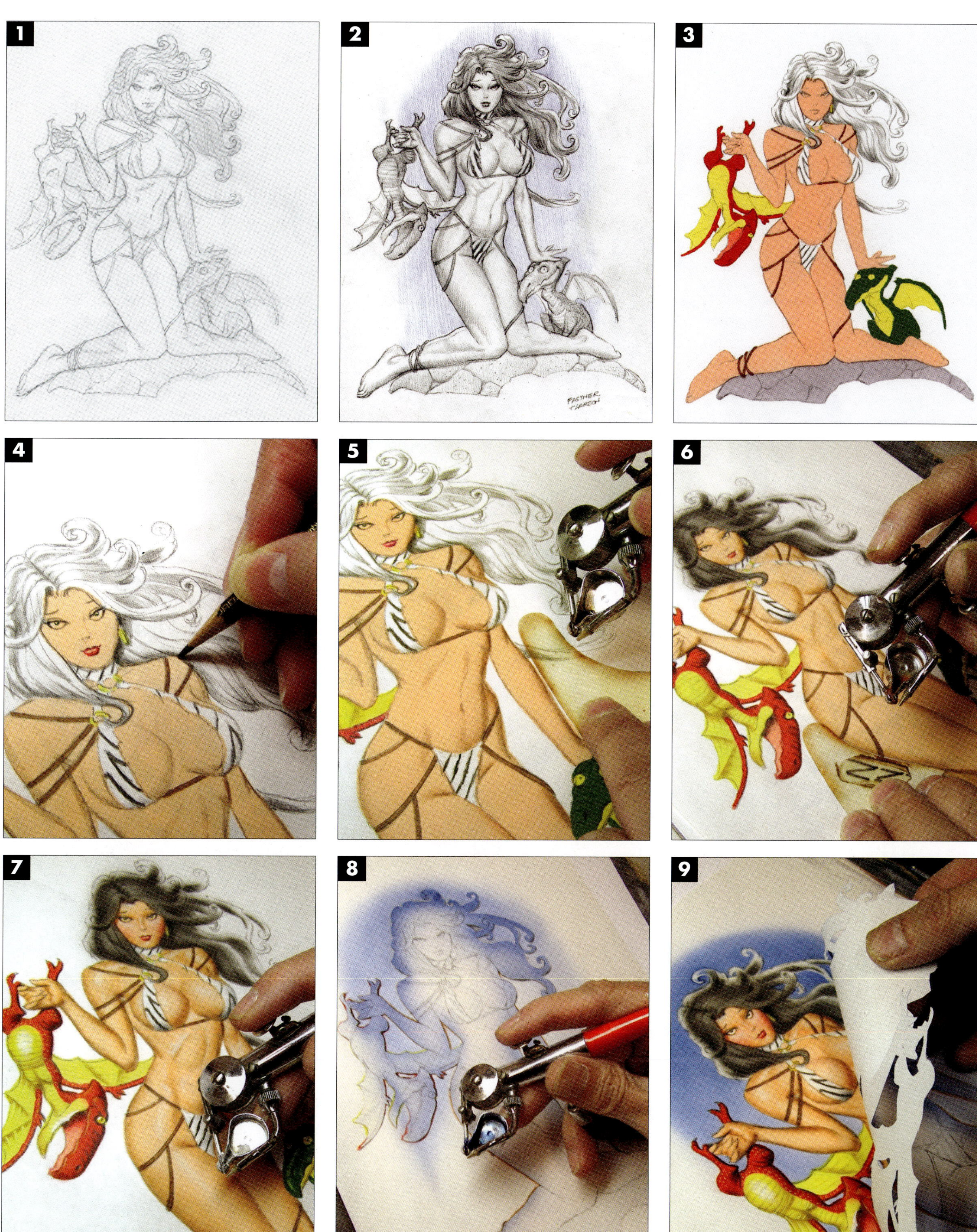

8) To spray the blue color for the background, Steve takes the remaining copy, and cuts the figures out with an X-acto knife. He sprays light coating of adhesive on the back of the cut out to create a paper mask, which is then placed over the already painted areas. He then sprays Badger blue paint onto the background.

9) The paper mask is removed. Steve then uses white gouache and a sable brush to paint in the white rim lighting around the edge of the girls' hair and skin, and on the dragons. Finishing touches, such as dark lines and other highlights, are added with watercolor, black ink, and gouache. The finished art is permanently mounted to a sheet of two ply illustration board for protection and durability.

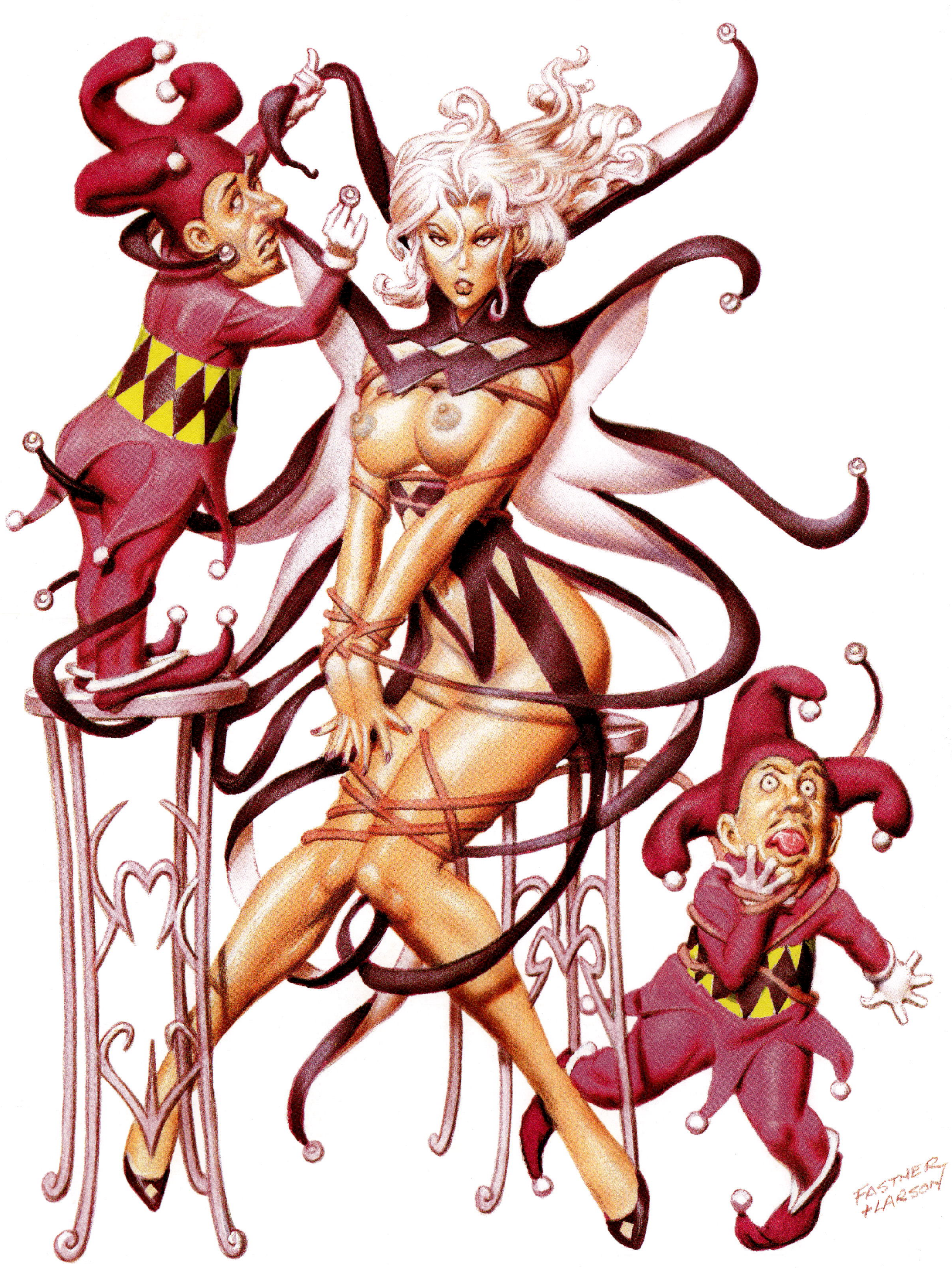

Belling the Cat